Pioneering the Kingdom

*Experiences in Applying the Apostolic Pattern
for a Sustainable Reproducible Mission*

Marc Carrier

Values-Driven

Acknowledgements

First and foremost, to our God and Father through our Lord and Savior Jesus Christ belongs all the glory for this work, and for all His rich and wonderful blessings on our journey in His service.

I'd like to acknowledge my wife Cindy, first for her willing partnership and steadfast support and encouragement through all of life's challenges, as well as her insight, heart, mastery of the art of writing, and scalpel for a pen, which have taken this content to higher levels. Your numerous hours of effort show, and are much appreciated. Thanks, sweetie!

I'd like to thank Glenn Roseberry, whose on-the-ground partnership in this mission has proven an immeasurable encouragement. Also, stateside mission director Bill VanHuss, whose counsel and support have kept us going through some of the darkest moments.

I would also like to thank brother Bruce Gordon, for his direct role in training and mobilizing me for foreign missions. I am positive I would not be here today if not for his influence.

I'd like to thank David Servant, whose comments during the review process of this book proved invaluable.

Finally, I would like to express my heartfelt appreciation for every brother and sister who has participated in this journey through direct influence, prayers, and financial support. Your collective support for us, and for this mission, has made it all possible.

Foreword

Everyone talks about discipleship and making disciples. But I have almost never met anyone that *has* a disciple. How many teachers, how many writers, how many pastors, can actually turn and say, *here are my disciples? Here are the men I am discipling.* And, *here are the men my disciples are discipling.* You hold in your hands *Pioneering the Kingdom*, a book by a man who actually has disciples. Those disciples are making disciples. I am not aware of any book like it.

I walked into a church one time here in Africa. The pastor was very excited to show me around. He showed me the new tin roof, the beautiful bunting they had on the walls for services. Great care was given each week to wash, iron, and hang them. You see, they wanted to look and be like the churches the Western workers were used to back home. He hoped and prayed for paned windows someday. After the grand tour, he beamed with pride and told me his joy over what the Lord had done in providing this wonderful building. I asked him, *where are your disciples*? He looked at me as though I asked him, *where is your spaceship*? He was no longer smiling.

Somehow we from the West had made an impression on this man about what the mission of the church was, and he wound up lavishing his attention on bunting and buildings. Making a nice meeting place was the focus of his weekly preparation, the object of his offerings, and the joy of his congregation. I realized how far from God's plan our understanding of the Great Commission and purpose of the Church had fallen. We had reproduced not disciples, not disciple-makers, but property managers.

In the West, perhaps we are not really sure what a *disciple* actually is. We have turned discipleship into a buzz word. We don't know how to make disciples, so we just take what we already do and we call it *discipleship*. Everyone that followed Jesus was asked to go and make disciples. But frankly, most don't have a clue as to what Jesus is talking about. We think it is a bible study or new teaching. Perhaps we think we are discipling when we teach to insure a believer is observing the same orthodoxy our group holds. (You know, make sure they have the correct doctrine.) Actually, *discipleship* is Jesus' own method of Kingdom expansion. This book was written with a vision for expanding the Kingdom of God according to this same method. I have walked with Marc for over five years, much of that time here in Africa. I can tell you, you hold in your hand a book by a man that actually makes and has disciples in multiple house churches in East Africa. I hope that excites you.

In my life time I have been around people that gather existing Christians into little groups, meet and study and say they are making disciples or are emphasizing discipleship. It is mostly rhetoric, or a change of rhetoric. We have no idea of how to actually call men to discipleship. We are not sure it is even necessary. We don't train them to obey Jesus's commands, a vital part of discipleship and part of the Great Commission. And we certainly don't know how to teach others to go and make disciples themselves. Marc Carrier has done these very things.

The lessons learned and experiences gained in order for Marc to be a disciple, make disciples, and train disciples to do the same were not easily acquired. The application of biblical principles in a new culture is fraught with challenges and discouragement. Marc has persevered through setbacks, betrayals, wrong turns, gossip, theft, threats, and illnesses. I have personally watched him overcome in a year, what most deal with in a lifetime. I am honored to have leadership that is paying the price to take people from the kingdom of darkness into the Kingdom of Light. It is not for the faint of heart to call men to become what Jesus meant them to be: agents of the Kingdom of God; disciples of the Lord Jesus Christ; men and women who have exchanged allegiance from all the folly of this world, to the God of eternity.

So, as a disciple, being discipled by a disciple-maker, I invite you to learn how to do the same. In this book you will find practical, actionable, and proven methods and practices in creating a multi-generational discipleship movement— just like Jesus taught. A plan to fill the earth with His glory! Not a theory, not just another book, not just a cool topic. No, here is a story of how one man and his family left the comfort of the West and embarked on an adventure to extend the Kingdom of God, as commanded by King Jesus.

Oh, to have had this from the start! What a treasure it would have been to have known what Marc knows now. *Pioneering the Kingdom* contains the stories, the practices, and the tools of a successful disciple-maker. I know this because I am being discipled by Marc Carrier. I am applying these methods. I have disciples that are making disciples. Not theories, not buzz words. Real multi-generational reproduction. Real Kingdom expansion. It is the book I always needed and wanted. I pray you read it. I pray you use it. I pray you are never the same. We are still learning. Still adapting and still growing. I hope you join us in expanding the Kingdom of God.

For His glory,

M. Glenn Roseberry, Jr.
Disciple, and missionary to East Africa

Introduction

You've probably picked up this book because you have an interest in foreign missions. However, this book is certainly not meant for everyone. *Pioneering the Kingdom* is specifically designed for field practitioners—those interested in engaging in mission work at home or abroad. In it, you'll read about my personal experiences as a pioneer missionary, with the ultimate goal of setting in motion a sustainable and reproducible Kingdom movement led by indigenous saints. By sharing my experiences alongside the teachings of the Scriptures and wisdom gleaned from other missiologists, I hope to equip future pioneer missionaries to fulfill their calling from the Lord.

However, even if you never make it to a foreign mission field, the practical advice on evangelism, discipleship, and church development may be utilized for the Lord's service right where you are. Although my story revolves around a foreign mission, you will recognize from my personal testimony that these principles are applicable everywhere because they are gleaned from Scripture and not simply from man's wisdom.

A pioneer missionary running off to the field before being prepared by God is going to encounter serious problems. In fact, you will see in my testimony that no matter how prepared you think you are, you will *still* encounter problems! Therefore, preparation at home prior to booking your flight should not be neglected, even if one has a sense of calling. I share my own experiences of preparation simply to emphasize their importance; however, the things God did in my life should not be construed as any type of "cookie cutter" approach. This is simply my testimony of God's work in my life.

In my days of preparation for the mission field, my personal growth experiences were of vital necessity. I also relied heavily on the works of several missiologists (many mentioned herein), but needed to read multiple volumes, in addition to the Bible, in order to put the pieces of the puzzle together. Some authors had experience in discipleship, which is an often-neglected element of both personal spiritual growth and church development. Others emphasized house church as an end in and of itself, neglecting the importance of raising up leaders who would make the movement sustainable and reproducible. Still others shared a biblical "recipe" for foreign missions work, but had never actually put their ideas into practice in the field. Finally, others varied so significantly on doctrine and the vital message, it seemed necessary to prepare a Kingdom-centric missions piece. I gleaned much from others' work, but there was nothing quite like *doing it* practically in the field to put the whole process into sharp perspective.

Intertwined with my trials and successes on the ground in Kenya, you will see the biblical basis behind it all. The four phases of a pioneer mission are evangelism (specifically, Luke 10 evangelism), discipleship, church development, and the Great Commandment works. As my story unfolds, you'll see how all these elements work in concert in a healthy pioneer mission.

It is my hope that this volume will prove to be a valuable resource for those seeking to answer the calling of God's service, either at home or in foreign places. We Westerners are all about "one-stop shopping," and this book has the potential to be all you need to set a sustainable, reproducible mission into motion.

Chapter 1: A Life Prepared

Every job comes with a set of qualifications that a candidate must meet. Some roles are more demanding than others. When it comes to becoming a pioneer missionary, biblical knowledge is a must, but it takes even more than an education; it takes experience.

I certainly didn't set out to become a pioneer missionary when I first started serving the Lord as a much younger, newly-married man. However, God has been faithful to use all of my experiences to equip me for the task, and has given me the faith to trust in His leading as He has opened the way for this adventure.

Cindy and I met during our senior year of high school; both of us had a church background and believed in God, but neither one of us had yet made a commitment to Christ. We married shortly after our graduation from college, and I worked crazy hours as a field scientist doing environmental remediation. I often traveled several hours a day, to and from job sites. I found myself listening to talk radio, and eventually Christian radio.

In one interview, someone explained that the Bible was inspired and authoritative. If you've been brought up in a Christian home, that is not a huge revelation. However, to me, a non-Christian who had lived a rebellious life without any absolutes, this was *unheard of*. That evening when I arrived at our apartment, I dusted off my Bible, dropped it on the dining room table with a resounding *thump*, and emphatically said to Cindy, "If this is true, we are going to live by it!"

That Sunday we went to a local, evangelical church service. We both silently prayed the altar call prayer and were Christians, as far as we understood. The pastor and elders of the church really took us under their wings and I ended up in several study groups, read many challenging books, and even took an apologetics course, all within our first year as Christians. However, we then moved to another town and thus had to find a new church.

Soon after we committed to a new local church, the pastor did something that would revolutionize our discipleship; he implemented small groups that met weekly in homes. The groups were organized geographically, and we were grouped together with four mature, Christian families. For about three years we met regularly, read and discussed the Scriptures, and spoke influence into each other's lives. Cindy and I were introduced to homeschooling for the first time; we saw what strong, biblical marriages looked like; we learned about child training and rearing from folks who had observable fruit. Sunday became more of a ritual, but Friday evenings were where we learned what it meant to be followers of Christ and literally abide by His Word.

As our spiritual growth progressed, my career was likewise taking off; this was a major blessing, as Cindy had permanently surrendered work when our first child was born. I went from field scientist, to project manager, to managing the largest program in the corporation in just five years. With the added income and a growing family, we finally succumbed to Cindy's Dad's desire that we buy Cindy's childhood home. With the move came the realization that we would need to find a new church yet again.

We ended up at a Pentecostal church with an energetic, young pastor that piqued our interest. We were challenged by a couple of their doctrinal positions, but went on to make it our church home for seven years. We were finally baptized there, both of us 26 years of age, in the frigid October waters of New England.

We had many in our church operating in the gifts of the Spirit: intercessors, prophets, evangelists and teachers. We met with several of them on a weekly basis for prayer, Bible study, worship, and mutual encouragement. Ironically, all of us had committed our lives to Christ in 1997, so we jokingly called ourselves, "The '97 Club."

At this time, the Lord began to guide my spiritual journey in a new direction. Our first child had been born via C-section due to Cindy's pregnancy-related hernia. Not long after our baptism, we discovered Cindy was expecting again, and the hernia re-occurred. During a special evening church service with a visiting evangelist and prophet, we all prayed for Cindy's healing and that the baby would be used for God's glory. Within a short time, the hernia simply went away. The second part of the prayer would have a spectacular fulfillment, though we didn't know it at the time.

When the baby, named Jonah, was born, all was fine during delivery. However, immediately after his birth, the nursing staff jumped into high gear and rushed him off because he failed to aspirate. We were left in the dark, but I snuck around and listened in on conversations; I saw doctors hold up a scan clearly showing nothing but a black mass in his chest cavity. In time, we were given the news: Jonah had a congenital diaphragmatic hernia. He was transported to a regional hospital in a bubble connected to many wires and tubes, before we even had a chance to touch him.

When we were left alone, Cindy and I prayed together and were given supernatural peace. Even with the horrible report of possible outcomes for Jonah, we knew for certain God was in control. Whatever the result was, we were willing to accept it. It may seem heartless to say that we were not emotional about what was going on; what parent wouldn't be? Yet God used some recent miraculous events in my life to encourage us and help us receive this news with strength and confidence in His perfect plan for us and for Jonah.

The morning after Jonah's birth, we were visited by our family in the hospital. A doctor from the regional university hospital called to give us the results of the extensive evaluation and testing they had performed. Jonah indeed had a congenital diaphragmatic hernia: a hole in the diaphragm that allows organs to move into the lung cavity. His complete small intestines were in his lung cavity. As a result, his lungs were under-developed and his heart was pushed clear to the right side of his body. The doctors reported an additional problem with his heart valves, and even a missing spleen and kidney! During my conversation with the doctor, he said that Jonah's current condition could very well be terminal. When I hung up the phone, I repeated to everyone exactly what I had been told. Immediately, numerous people began to cry.

At that pivotal moment, our pastor arrived. We relayed the grim report, and he responded, "I've seen God move in situations like these." Quietly, a sobbing family member whispered under her breath, "But He won't!" Cindy and I were soon left alone, still experiencing God's peace. In our private conversations together, I told Cindy, "Better that this happened to us than to someone else; God knows, we are equipped to handle it."

As we resolved this, immediately the Lord spoke to me very clearly in my spirit: "Since you are willing to accept whatever I give you, I will give you my best." The Lord added another message, *"All the parts are there, and they all work."* At that moment, I knew that Jonah would be healed.

Surgery revealed that, despite being crowded by intestines, the lungs were actually pink and developed. That in itself was unexpected for the surgeon. Even more amazing? *All the parts were there, and they all worked*! With much animation and with a look of amazement, the surgeon reported to us, "I reached down and under with my pinky and I TOUCHED IT! The kidney—it was THERE!"

Our joy with the news of what God had done attracted the attention of some staff nurses, who solemnly warned us that the road to recovery was still long and there were no guarantees of the outcome just yet. In fact, Jonah was again transferred to a higher level hospital in case an ECMO (heart and lung bypass machine) would be needed.

Surprising all the nurses who cared for him, Jonah rapidly recovered and came home three weeks after his birth, despite conservative best estimates of several months. A visiting nurse came to check up on Jonah during the first week in July, after our first weekend out of the hospital. She expressed amazement with how well he was doing, certain that there would be ongoing complications. She asked Cindy, "When was his surgery?"

"The eleventh."

"Of *June*?"

Cindy affirmed the date, to which the nurse responded,

"One of my co-workers takes care of a little boy with this condition who needs 18 hours per day of care!"

Cindy asked, "Why isn't he in the hospital?"

"Because he's in kindergarten!"

The nurse gave Jonah a clean bill of health and he has never experienced any complications since his discharge from the hospital.

I've used many keystrokes to detail the events surrounding Jonah's miraculous healing to illustrate a very important aspect of God preparing me for the mission field. I wasn't necessarily lacking in biblical knowledge; what I needed was experience seeing God intervene in the natural. Through the experience, I learned that God is not confined to the covers of a leather-bound book. He is alive, active, and still doing the things we read about in our Bibles. God can do anything, and He does what He says He will do! God knew that I would need this kind of faith to keep me stable during the often-turbulent times of pioneer missions.

I also learned to hear God's quiet voice. Before this, I can't say that I could confidently discern what was from Him and what was from me. Yet Jesus said, according to our faith will it be done to us (see Matthew 9:29), and that we are to walk by faith, not by sight (see 2 Corinthians 5:7). If God had not prepared me in this training ground, I would never have stepped out in faith when I knew He was calling me to the mission field. This strength of faith is vital in the spiritual growth of any aspiring missionary.

Nearly all Christians believe that the Bible is inspired and authoritative. However, many think the miraculous events recorded therein are somehow not for us today. Sure, charismatics expect God's intervention. Yet we often learn about a God who wrote a book and fail to hear from and see the works of that God manifested in the natural. God becomes distant and sterile if His Word was meant to simply show us how to live. At least, that was my experience before these miraculous events. However, afterwards I found my understanding of God transformed. I became very aware of His presence and power and His personal involvement in my life.

At the same time, I would caution anyone who is learning to discern God's voice: He will never speak in contradiction to His written Word. I have seen many a professing Christian emphatically say that their biblically-condemned actions are somehow uniquely sanctioned for them because of some special revelation from the Holy Spirit. That is the height of foolishness. God is a God of order, and will never contradict Himself. Yet contra-wise, I see others deny God's personal role and activity in the lives of modern Christians. On the mission field, many of these become believers in God's power by necessity when confronted with the demon-possessed, witchcraft and spiritual warfare, and the sick and dying. Studying about God is not enough. We need His direct intervention!

For me, the manifestation of God's specific interaction and power in my life has resulted in even more confidence in, and therefore obedience to, His Word. I know His Words are no fairy tale. His promises are true. And even if I fail to understand the "why" of some things, I know with confidence that He knows what is best and obedience is always prescribed. Therefore, never wait for a "sign" when He has already clearly spoken His will in Scripture. But when He does speak, listen carefully and act upon His guidance.

For this reason, a very clear and distinct word from the Lord should be part of one's calling to the mission field. Absent this, the Enemy can bring doubt, and discouragement or even depression can derail the mission. Yet faith allows one to weather any storm and brings clarity to God's vision in moments of need.

After the healing of Jonah, my passion and enthusiasm for sharing Christ with others caught up with my insatiable desire to learn about God. At that time, a mature brother in our church attended a week-long, "train-the-trainer" evangelism program. I attended a shorter version of the same training. Together, we immediately launched an evangelism program in our church; I was the designated "field trainer." I began leading many people to Christ (not in a way I would approve of today, but a step in the right direction).

Even at work, I was "on mission." I led numerous administrative staff and professionals to Christ and hosted a weekly Bible study in my office during lunch hour. The Lord intervened to protect me when my job was threatened as a result. The program I managed thrived, even as God continued to expose me to the practical skills I would need to evangelize, make disciples, and oversee a future mission of numerous churches in multiple countries.

I had become a program manager at work, leading a large team of professionals: project managers, scientists, engineers and field staff. It was in this environment that I learned about managing staff, much the hard way: interviewing and hiring, training and mentoring, evaluations and reviews, matching talents with the tasks…yes, even correcting employees and releasing those who under-performed. Working with the challenges of constant under-staffing and case over-load, I also learned how to optimize a program by introducing efficiencies and management tools. I didn't know it at the time, but these experiences would prepare me for the work God had in store for me.

In the church, Cindy and I remained active and I was invited to be an advisor to our pastor; since our denomination did not have elders. Our family had grown to five children and Cindy had also begun homeschooling. Our homeschooling and conviction about parental discipleship of children set us apart in our mainstream evangelical church, where we eventually withdrew from the children's church program and had our children participate in the worship service with us. However, our marriage was strong and our convictions were firm. Without that foundation, we never would have made it through those first hard years abroad.

So, my advice to those feeling a missionary call also includes this admonition: get your household in order before you head out. The emotional toll faced by the nuclear family will put all but the very strongest of marriages to the test. I can't count the number of times I've been down, yet my wife has been a source of encouragement, or has provided a different perspective that has made all the difference. Likewise, when she has been struggling, I have prayed for her and tried to be of practical help and encouragement. It is by the Lord's grace that we have rarely both been "down" at the same time, as we have been each other's anchor through the vicissitudes of life on the mission field.

Interestingly, I recently perused a study on long-term missionaries[1] that included a list of the three factors that most hinder missionaries from achieving their field objectives: lack of finances, family issues, and relationship problems. Additionally, length of service is related to both marital contentment and previous ministry experience in a local church. These conclusions point to the importance of both "at-home preparations" (being involved in the Lord's work prior to being "sent"), and focusing on family relationships as a prerequisite for long-term, foreign service.

We'll get into the "at-home preparations" a bit more in the next chapter. As you can see up to this point, the Lord had already been taking me through sufficient experiences in my personal life that I was adding to my knowledge, faith, and engaging in the first of the four phases of sustainable reproducible missions: evangelism. I was also growing in the practical skills related to management that would serve me well as a pioneer missionary in the future. I was working my way through some very practical experiences—and God had much more in store for me!

---

[1] *US Report of Findings on Missionary Retention*, December 2003. Accessed at http://www.worldevangelicals.org/resources/rfiles/res3_95_link_1292358708.pdf on March 3, 2016.

Chapter 2: Experience at Home

Reading *The Insanity of Obedience*, the truth of this particular quote resonated with me:

> Perhaps serving the cause of Christ overseas can seem glamorous and even exotic. Perhaps people feel more open in sharing a personal testimony in environments where they are not known...and where they will not be around long enough to reveal personal character. On the other hand, perhaps a brief time overseas can be used by God to renew a commitment at home, or to focus a person's attention on ministry close at hand. Perhaps. But the practice of going thousands of miles from home while neglecting lost, needy, and nearby neighbors points to a believing life that is badly out of balance. Christ has commanded all of His followers to incarnate Him wherever they happen to be. Neglecting "Jerusalem" threatens to undermine the entire mission endeavor. Ministry among the Nations simply must be a natural extension of whatever ministry is happening at home. Being a poured-out and broken vessel among the people we know best is essential preparation—even more, it is a prerequisite—for ministry among people we do not yet know. And the kind of maturity and seasoning that comes from extended ministry at home tends to reduce the mistakes that we are all prone to make in mission settings.

> God help us if we attempt to do in faraway places things that we would never dream of doing close to home! (Nik Ripken, *The Insanity of Obedience*)

This is something God brought me to see personally during my own preparation and subsequent field work, so I've emphasized it over the years in conversations with folks curious about the mission field. I say it like this: if you think ministering to someone in a vastly different culture, who speaks a different language, is somehow easier than speaking to your own people in your own nation, you deceive yourself. If you rush to the mission field, you might make converts, but never disciples. If you have never preached the Kingdom, taken someone through surrender and repentance, baptized them, and mentored them to obedience to Christ, if you have never started a single new home fellowship, *don't purchase the ticket*. First, get to work with your own people.

You say you don't know how? I can understand that. There are precious few non-institutional training resources or programs available for sincere apostolic candidates to benefit from. That is just one of the reasons this book was written: as a starting point for the pioneer missionary. Though I do not agree with *everything* from just about any book or ministry, I would still encourage any aspiring missionary to read *Reproducible Pastoral Training* by Patrick O'Connor and *Contagious Disciple Making* by David and Paul Watson. If you want to learn about the Kingdom of God, read *The Kingdom that Turned the World Upside Down* by David Bercot. If your interest is multi-generational discipleship, look up www.KeystoneProject.org. Home fellowship? Try *The Church in the House* by Robert Fitts. For a crash course in everything related to Kingdom missions, visit our website www.KingdomDriven.org. But as I've said, knowledge is just a small part of field preparedness; personal ministry experience is where you will develop skills and be proven for what God means for you to do.

Whether on the foreign mission field or at home, when it comes to discipleship, *you can't take someone where you have never been.* To use an old cliché, *apples don't fall far from the tree.* If you have not experienced complete surrender to Christ, truly repented of your sins, been baptized, and begun to walk in the holiness and obedience that leads to eternal life, you cannot make someone else authentically experience those same things. If you have not counted the cost, if you are not willing to endure hardship like a good soldier of Christ, then your disciples will likewise be weak in these areas. If you do not have a vibrant devotional life of prayer, fasting, and discernment in hearing the voice of God, neither will your potential disciples. And only God, with time, can bring you through the experiences needed to grow you in these ways.

If you experience personal weaknesses in any of these areas, the mission field will not strengthen you; it will only reveal the weaknesses. If you feel the calling of God, start doing hard ministry where you are. Visit the nearest shelter or inner city setting and step into a culture different from your own. Experience the challenges, setbacks, betrayals and hardships associated with work that might be out of your comfort zone. Prove your field-worthiness where you are, before expecting God to call you to the foreign mission field. I experienced many things in my life that were a must for an aspiring missionary, but I wish I had been better prepared for these cultural challenges, in particular.

Thus, if you do receive a Word from the Lord about serving in a foreign location, study your anticipated environment: language, culture, climate, security, diseases, medical care, diet, pests, transportation, home management, shopping, education, and so on. Make alterations to your home life as much as practicable for the upcoming changes. Our family adjusted to a staple-food-only diet for six months prior to our move. We studied the language, researched and prepared as much as possible, and it was still a very challenging transition.

In your zeal for foreign missions, do not expect that the Lord will call you without equipping you locally for what you will face abroad. As I've already shared a bit, in my early Christian walk, the Lord gave me much opportunity to share the gospel and deal with opposition to my faith.

In fact, in the home and in my workplace, God continued to build all the skills and personal attributes I would need in order to better serve Him later in life. Just when I could have gotten comfortable with my successes in climbing the corporate ladder, the Lord began to nudge me in another direction. I saw that I had been committing my best time and talents in endeavors that lacked eternal significance. My impending eight-year anniversary in the environmental industry was a major milestone, as I would be eligible to receive two advanced professional certifications. I feared becoming entrenched in my career and never moving on to something more meaningful.

At that time, a brother at church was seeking a mature project manager to take his company to the next level. I saw this as the Lord's will and made the move, though it meant shifting to a completely different industry, at a significant pay cut.

I jumped in and learned the field, receiving multiple professional certifications in the new disciplines as well as in project management. In this job, besides project management duties, I was tasked with training development and instructor-led training. Being an introvert, this was quite a bit out of my comfort zone. Yet, as I mastered a command of the material I was teaching, I quickly grew comfortable and even learned to enjoy public teaching.

In my training development role, I also learned to take vast amounts of material on complex subjects and organize and deliver it in bite-sized chunks, both orally and in written form, in a style that was intuitive and easy-to-understand. This would later be instrumental in the development of the field manuals we use in the mission.

During the first year after I transitioned to the new company, the Lord had really been urging me to write down everything He was revealing to me through His Word and the Holy Spirit concerning discipling and training children. I did what I could, taking notes when I was not at work, but I grew more and more uncomfortable with not doing what I knew God wanted me to do. One night, the Lord gave me a very clear vision of the book He wanted me to write. The experience with Jonah's miraculous healing gave me crystal clarity of His voice, so I knew the time to do it was "now." Cindy and I discussed the vision, and in a step of faith, I put my two weeks' notice in at work that day.

In the natural, it was absolute foolishness. We had bills to pay and no savings; I even cut up our credit cards because I didn't want the illusion of credit to sustain us. We were likewise determined not to use government programs or tell people of our needs. We trusted exclusively on God through prayer, and I would have to say that was one of the most remarkable times in our faith journey. God miraculously provided for our family every step of the way.

At one point, we had just $13 in the bank and Cindy was crying because we had no fruit for the children. During her time of prayer, God spoke to her and told her that just so she knew it was Him and not her husband asking her to go through this, He would grant her request. A relative arrived at the door with some leftover fruit almost immediately. Days later, we were out of fruit again, and Cindy cried to the Lord once more. The Lord repeated that He would bless her, but this time through an unbeliever. Shortly after, an unbelieving family member arrived with a large bag of fruit, unsolicited—and he had not even been informed that I had quit my job! I thanked him and asked him why he had done this great deed. He looked at me very bewildered and simply said, "I don't know."

From that time on, there was little doubt that God would provide, and we saw Him do just that through seven months of my unemployment. During that period, not only were our daily needs met, but we cleared our student loan debt, purchased a nearly-new, 15-passenger van in cash, and consistently gave financially toward the Lord's work.

This was certainly a boost to my faith, giving me confidence in God's provision—a must on the mission field, of course. Writing a book during this time also honed my skills in communication and publication, gifts that God would continue to use in the future.

After completing the book, I returned to work (this time, remotely from home, since the base office had moved farther away). I also felt led to begin releasing from our local fellowship. This was a process, as I had leadership responsibilities that I wanted to honor. The Lord also gave me a clear vision that He wanted us to move to central Indiana. That was odd, considering that we knew no one there and had never even visited the state. Regardless, we prepared for the inevitable.

In time, we left our church with blessing, but our imminent move had still not finalized. A family-integrated church was on our hearts from the Lord, but the only such fellowship we could find in our area was a home fellowship—not something we were looking for at the time, but something that God meant for us to experience. Even as knowledgeable as I was of the Scriptures, it had escaped my notice that there were no church buildings spoken of in the New Testament, and that services were interactive, participatory, and Spirit-led.

We also noted how the families boasted strong marriages and family relationships, well-behaved children, modest dress, an aversion towards worldly entertainment, and many other characteristics that appealed to where we were at that point in our spiritual walk. In fact, the meetings were very reminiscent of the small group we attended for our earliest few years as believers that were so instrumental in our personal spiritual growth. We attended that fellowship for a mere seven months, but developed a bond with those folks the likes of which were comparable to our several years in the prior church.

Even more significantly, right before we moved to Indiana, a missionary with experience working with Muslims in Asia moved to our small town, and we providentially crossed paths. These mature believers were also house-churchers and homeschoolers. This brother was the first apostolically-gifted, Spirit-led individual that I had extensive interaction with. The discipleship that he and his wife invested in Cindy and me was instrumental to the future plans that God had for us.

That August, Cindy and I independently received confirmation from the Lord that we would soon be moving to Indiana. I was on a business trip in Illinois when the Lord spoke to me and said the buyer would come imminently. In fact,

He said I would move at the end of the month. I called Cindy, and she confirmed she had received the same message. I asked my employer for the last week of September and the first week of October off to move to Indiana. She asked if I had received an offer on the house yet. I told her no, but that God told me it was imminent. Lo and behold, we closed on September 29! At the last minute, we found the perfect house in Indiana and closed on it in 48 hours during transit. We had never set eyes on the house, yet we knew it was the Lord's will, and it was indeed perfect for our needs at that time.

After our move, my missionary brother continued to flood me with books and websites on house church planting, discipleship, and missionary work. My philosophy of house church changed dramatically. The house church we had been introduced to in Connecticut was wonderful, yet it was more of a "holy huddle," attracting like-minded people who were already spiritually mature. The resources my new mentor was sharing with me emphasized the house church as the optimal vehicle for evangelism, Kingdom expansion, and discipleship. That concept revolutionized my thinking.

We linked up with an existing house church in Indiana and, with another gifted brother, began adding both disciples and fellowships. The fellowships were a mix of new converts and others who were disenchanted with their traditional churches for various reasons. We fellowshipped for several years in these house churches. Cindy and I continued writing and publishing Christian books; we also began speaking and exhibiting at regional homeschool conventions. In that environment, we encountered many like-minded folks. This was where, again, the Lord dramatically intervened in my faith journey.

We began to feel as though it was time to move on from the home fellowships we had been a part of. The closest fellowship to us was still some distance away, which was very limiting for ongoing relationships outside of Sunday fellowship. Even more importantly, I was delving deeper into missiology at that time, due to my continued interactions with the apostolically-gifted brother from Connecticut. (Specifically, I was learning from the likes of George Patterson and David Watson.) I was feeling the desire to stretch my wings and try out some of the church-planting methods I was only reading about—particularly Luke 10 evangelism.

We gently loosened our ties with our existing house church group, and I went out into our community looking for a "man of peace." (More on this Luke 10 evangelism method in a future chapter.) Canvassing the neighborhood, a man and his teenage son who lived on our street expressed interest in the Gospel and ended up being baptized (in another neighbor's hot tub!). A couple other local people interested in house church ended up crossing our paths in other ways, and suddenly we had a fellowship meeting in our home!

One Friday in the summer, Cindy took the children (all seven of them at the time) out to run errands and enjoy some time at the library. It was noon by the time they came back into our little town, and they made a last stop at the post office. As you can imagine, it had been a tiring morning and Cindy wasn't really looking forward to going home and making lunch for everyone. Coincidentally, the post master said, "Hey! You should bring all the kids across the street to the Lion's Club. They're serving lunch today, no strings attached. I think it's hot dogs. The kids'll love it!" Somehow Cindy had a feeling this was a "God thing," so she went.

When they entered the building, they were warmly welcomed by Mike, who brought them to a table and then sat with them for several minutes making small talk. His conversation was peppered with praise to God, mention of prayer, and so on. Cindy's spiritual radar was up, so she guided the conversation with some questions, discovering more about Mike's spiritual condition, his church history, and his family. By the time they left, Cindy had extended an invitation for Mike to bring his wife to our home for dinner sometime, and she had taken his phone number so I could get in contact with him. Ultimately, Mike and his wife also became a part of our home fellowship.

At that time, God was also nudging us about walking in greater obedience to His Word—specifically, pursuing the Kingdom of God rather than the Kingdom of the world, and being willing to literally sell everything if that was what God asked. We put our house on the market, as we realized it was more than we needed. We lived in a small town with a population of 679 people, distant from any employment centers, and owned a very nice house on a very private ten acres. The market for our house was non-existent. However, we began selling and giving away our possessions, in hopes that "someday" we would move (and downsize). To where, we were not sure—but God already had a plan we knew nothing about.

As it turned out, all these steps we were taking to simplify were in good timing, as the economy tanked and my job went away. It was no surprise, as the Lord forewarned me in August that my job would be ending in December. His exact message was that I was being "thrust from the nest," and it was time to fly. At that time, I called my employer and of course was assured that this was not the case. Even so, I found out in November that my job would end at the end of the month.

Just weeks after becoming unemployed, I was invited to Kenya to teach on many of the practical materials highlighted in our books. I prayed in earnest and determined that this was, indeed, the Lord's will. While in Kenya, the theme of my teachings naturally flowed from practical disciplines to evangelism, discipleship and, ultimately, home fellowship. The teachings were enthusiastically received, but I had no idea at the time of the cultural dynamics of a white person visiting Africa. It would only be much later that we would learn that this was normal treatment for all foreign visitors.

While up at night in western Kenya, the Lord gave me a vision I will never forget. I'll spare you the details, but the message was clear: we were to move to Kenya. I called Cindy that evening and before I could say anything, she asked, "We are moving there, aren't we?" She had received the same message. That was mind-bending for both of us, since up to this point, foreign missions were never even a remote consideration. Though a prophetic sister in the Lord (one of the "'97 Club") had previously spoken to me of an apostolic gifting on my life, I hadn't given it much thought. But now the Lord was clear: Kenya was in our future.

During these years, many of my experiences were important preparations for the mission field. Perhaps the most significant was the paradigm shift we experienced, from institutional church to house church. As I said, I had simply not seen it in Scripture before—but certainly, it was there. Actually experiencing it was eye-opening, and I would carry these lessons forward with me into Kenya, when the time finally came.

Since this is such a defining teaching with global applications (particularly important in persecuted environments where institutional church buildings would be not only impractical, but dangerous), let's talk about it a bit.[2] Jumping ahead of phase two of a mission (discipleship), church development constitutes the third phase of the pioneer missions process.

Modern church practices have deviated so very far from the New Testament ideal, it is challenging even to describe the New Testament church model using common English words. That is because the words themselves conjure a mental image far different from the simple Greek sense employed in the primitive church. For example, with the word *church*, we think of a building or a denomination. However, the Greek word that we translate as "church" is *ekklesia*, and it has a very specific meaning: *the called-out ones*.

Verses such as Colossians 1:13-14 and Ephesians 2:1-2 demonstrate that in Christ we are *called out* from Satan, sin and the world, and transferred *into* Christ's Kingdom. Citizens of this Kingdom—the people themselves—are the *church*. When you are fulfilling the Great Commission (which is to make disciples), you are indeed church-planting, because the people *are* the *church*—those who have been called out as the people of God:

> [4] And coming to Him as to a living stone which has been rejected by men, but is choice and precious in the sight of God, [5] you also, as living stones, are being

---

[2] These teachings are covered in Kingdom Driven Ministries' fourth teaching booklet, *What Does the Bible Say About Church?*, at www.KingdomDriven.org/Kingdom-resources.)

built up as a spiritual house for a holy priesthood, to offer up spiritual sacrifices acceptable to God through Jesus Christ. [9] But you are A CHOSEN RACE, A royal PRIESTHOOD, A HOLY NATION, A PEOPLE FOR *God's* OWN POSSESSION, so that you may proclaim the excellencies of Him who has called you out of darkness into His marvelous light; [10] for you once were NOT A PEOPLE, but now you are THE PEOPLE OF GOD; you had NOT RECEIVED MERCY, but now you have RECEIVED MERCY. (1 Peter 2; see also Ephesians 2:19-21)

Need I restate the obvious? We *are* the church! A special building or some named organization does not constitute a church. The people—the membership who have surrendered to Christ, repented, been baptized and made citizens of God's Kingdom by being born again—constitute the true church.

So, if the church is the people, and not a building, where did they meet? In houses, of course! Several New Testament verses acknowledge various house churches and those who are recognized as hosting them (see, for example, Colossians 4:15, Romans 16:3-5, 1 Corinthians 16:19, and Philemon 1-2).

Without any doubt, the churches that Paul planted exclusively met in the private homes of the disciples. Never is there a mention of a special religious building in the New Testament for Christian worship. While it is true that the Temple and other public buildings were centers for targeted evangelism, subsequent teaching and fellowship occurred in believers' homes. The institutional tradition would not begin for hundreds of years.

This understanding of *church* makes church planting simple and affordable, because people already have homes! This is especially necessary in developing nations, where adopting Western practices, like church buildings and programs, often presents limitations because of financial constraints. But church in a house is not just about the location. What they do in that house is even more important. What does a house church look like? The Bible tells us that, too:

[26] ...When you assemble, each one has a psalm, has a teaching, has a revelation, has a tongue, has an interpretation. Let all things be done for edification. [27] If anyone speaks in a tongue, *it should be* by two or at the most three, and *each* in turn, and one must interpret; [28] but if there is no interpreter, he must keep silent in the church; and let him speak to himself and to God. [29] Let two or three prophets speak, and let the others pass judgment. [30] But if a revelation is made to another who is seated, the first one must keep silent. [31] For you can all prophesy one by one, so that all may learn and all may be exhorted; [32] and the spirits of prophets are subject to prophets; [33] for God is not *a God* of confusion but of peace, as in all the churches of the saints. (1 Corinthians 14)

This may come as a shock to you, but New Testament church "services" did not boast a singled-out, salaried, professional teacher or preacher standing behind a pulpit. Fellowships were not human-led; rather, they were guided by humans and directed by the Holy Spirit. Upon the leading of the Holy Spirit, disciples would share a prophesy, a teaching, a song—whatever He directed. I know this is a radical departure from current Christian tradition; however, it is apostolic tradition. This is the foundation we are to use, lest we ignore the foundation of the apostles and prophets (see Ephesians 2:19-22).

An interactive service is vital for many reasons. I noted in my testimony that the small group we attended during our early Christian years proved more significant for our personal discipleship than attending traditional church service ever could. Likewise, we grew closer and developed deeper and stronger relationships with the saints in our first house church in just seven months than we had in several years in traditional church. This is because interaction promotes growth, in personal relationships and in the church.

The command and purpose of church is *discipleship*, not necessarily corporate worship. Worship is a way of life, walking in obedience to Christ and loving your fellow man—it is not a weekly Sunday event. Each of us has been prepared to receive and operate in spiritual gifts for the edification of the body; this is done in a house church environment that is participatory. Mutual accountability, public confession, and partaking in the Lord's Supper are all commonplace in a biblical home fellowship.

God was gracious to lead and teach me these things through my experiences and my mentors during my period of apprenticeship in the faith. I had a solid understanding of, and experience with, evangelism and planting house churches. I had most of the pieces of the puzzle in place, but as you'll see, putting it all together on the mission field still wasn't a seamless or simple endeavor.

Chapter 3: Setting our Sights on Kenya

Cindy and I both knew that we would be moving to Kenya, but it was also obvious that the time was not at hand. Little did I know, it would be three more long years of preparation before we finally got on the plane! God, in His wisdom, knew how much I was missing before I would even be close to ready. Even so, that calling began to shape our decision-making from that point forward.

The three years it took to prepare us for the mission field were even more important than all the previous years, in terms of our personal spiritual development. The lessons learned became vital in my continuing personal training.

Inasmuch as we had long been sincere believers with a desire to please God and obey His word, I admit there were still some subjects that produced *cognitive dissonance* in us. We read the Scriptures and saw what was written; then we saw the modern church, and how people lived in direct disregard of so much clear teaching. The home fellowship environment allowed us to delve deeper into the Scriptures and honestly discuss the challenging passages with other mature brethren without disturbing the *status quo*. Yet as we did just that, we realized how much farther we, ourselves, needed to go.

When I returned from my trip to Africa, the experience had left a lasting impact on me. During my time there, I was being taught as much as I was teaching. Short-term missions can impact people this way, and it certainly impacted me; however, it wasn't just the environment, it was the teachings themselves. The Lord was guiding me in what to teach others, and those teachings revolutionized my commitment to abide by the very same things. I came back energized to make our Indiana home fellowships more intentional in obeying Jesus and fulfilling the Great Commission.

I began by organizing a mini-conference on the things I had been teaching in Kenya. Some of it revolved around the house church teachings I was reading at the time; yet at a deeper level, some "missing elements," such as surrender and total commitment, were also brought to the forefront. I taught all day; at the end of the meeting our host told me that she had only heard such teachings from one other person before. She said, "You really need to meet him!" I saw this as a divine appointment and almost immediately decided to attend a one-week seminar hosted by this respected missionary trainer in South Dakota. His teachings proved invaluable.

Though up to that point, my studies of church planting had all taught both discipleship and obedience to Jesus, I must admit that I had glossed over those points in favor of the house church angle. Yet this next-level training put the emphasis squarely on multi-generational discipleship. The trainer would say, "Christ commanded us to make disciples; He said *He* would build His church!" Ah! I saw that I had put the cart before the horse. The church *is* the people. Our job is to bring people to surrender to Christ, repent, and be born again…and then teach them to obey Jesus. These "called out" people *are* the church. Of course, as I later implemented all four phases of pioneer missions in Kenya, I saw how each part works toward the development of the whole experience, but at this time my focus was on the necessity of discipleship in what I would say is the second phase.

These teachings on discipleship were very valuable in shaping my thoughts regarding missions; I began to think in terms of *quality* rather than *quantity* of disciples. Yet even if we focus on quality, the quantity also eventually happens! Look with me at what can actually be achieved through a discipleship process (this is excerpted from my previously published *Keys to Kingdom Expansion*)[3] and loosely based on the training that I attended at that time:

Let's compare an "evangelist" (defined as someone who leads someone in repeating a prayer after them and then sends them to church) with a "disciple-maker" (defined as someone who preaches the gospel of the Kingdom, brings them to surrender and repentance, baptizes them, and then teaches them to obey all that Jesus commanded). Assume the evangelist leads one person per day to repeat the "sinner's prayer" as compared to a disciple-maker making one disciple (obedient follower of Christ) per year. At the end of year one, the score is evangelist 366, disciples two; year two, evangelist 731, disciples four; year three, 1,096 to eight; year five, 1,826 to 32; year 10, 3,651 to 1,024; year 20, evangelist 7,301, and 1,048,576 obedient disciples. The entire world population would be reached in just 33 years, presuming making just one disciple per year. Are you with me on this?

Now you can understand why Jesus invested most of His effort in teaching and training just 12 individuals—because He knew that if He imparted Himself in those 12 (ultimately 11) men, the world would be turned upside down. If Jesus were ministering today, He would probably be considered a failure. He had no building, no named ministry, no salary, and just 12 "members." What a loser, right? Except, He knew what He was doing. We are the ones who are clueless! We design and execute our ministries with total disregard for the clear command and example of our Lord and Shepherd.

If Christians would accept the responsibility for obeying this teaching, we could reach the world for Christ in short order. Not all people are missionaries, but all Christians are commanded to observe all that Jesus commanded, which includes personally making disciples.

Needless to say, after soaking in teachings like these, I went home excited to share a new perspective with our house church network. Yet my enthusiasm was met with not a little bit of resistance. Not everyone was willing to truly surrender to Christ and pursue the life of obedience that His teachings demand. Unfortunately, even fewer shared my passion for Kingdom expansion.

---

[3] *Keys to Kingdom Expansion* is freely available at www.Kingdomdriven.org/Kingdom-resources.

Then the Lord took me even deeper. I had always been committed to a literal obedience to Christ's teachings. Yet the cultural Christian witness all around us implied that Jesus' teachings were optional; no one could answer the questions we ourselves had about some of Jesus' clear teachings, which were simply explained away. Then—it happened! We found fellowship at last.

We continued to exhibit and speak on the Midwest homeschool convention circuit that Spring as we had done in previous years. As God would have it, our booth that year was right next to an Anabaptist book seller. After conversing with the guy, he gave me a copy of *The Kingdom that Turned the World Upside Down*. I also purchased another informative book off of one of his racks. Between the two, a whole new world was opened to us.

We proceeded to read about the Ante-Nicene (AN) witness and other "Kingdom" Christians through history who voluntarily and willingly identified with and obeyed the literal teachings of Jesus Christ. We were not crazy after all! Jesus' teachings were indeed meant to be obeyed and thousands of men and women throughout history had sacrificed all to do just that. This was a monumental revelation. With renewed zeal, I read and studied the early church and Anabaptist history, finding there innumerable witnesses to this amazingly simple truth.

Within the AN writings we discovered that the gospel itself was one of the casualties of the theologians. This discovery forced us to revisit what it was that was proclaimed in the New Testament. For years we were left wondering why so many doctrines rested heavily on certain passages of Scripture, while totally ignoring or talking circles around others. The AN witness, however, did not ignore any Scripture, but rather upheld the whole of God's counsel in a seamless and intuitive way. Our cognitive dissonance was finally gone. Praise the Lord!

So what is the gospel of the Kingdom? If you ask someone what Christianity is about, the stock answer will be something like, "God's redemptive plan for humanity." But Jesus only mentioned dying on the cross for our sins a handful of times. He mentioned our need to be born again just once. He discussed being sent as a ransom once. He only mentioned church twice. So what did the lion's share of Jesus' teachings discuss? You guessed it: *the Kingdom of God*. The Kingdom of God is mentioned about 100 times in the New Testament. You'll notice that most of Jesus' parables start with, "The Kingdom of God may be compared to...," and then He tells a story.

In fact, Jesus said He was sent to Earth to proclaim the Kingdom of God! (Luke 4:43). What Jesus sent His disciples to do was exactly what He had been doing (Luke 9:2, Mark 4:23 and Matthew 9:35). Jesus explicitly stated that the end of the world would not come *until the gospel of the Kingdom* was preached to all nations (Matthew 24:14). That is exactly what His followers proceeded to do after His death and resurrection (Acts 8:12, 28:23 and 30-31). In fact, the establishment of this Kingdom on Earth was what Jesus commanded His followers to pray for (Matthew 6:10, Luke 11:2). The culmination of God's work is the fulfillment of this prayer (Revelation 11:15).

In my opinion, the best passage to summarize the gospel of the Kingdom is Colossians 1:13-14: "For He rescued us from the domain of darkness, and transferred us to the Kingdom of His beloved Son, in whom we have redemption, the forgiveness of sins." In essence, we all start off as enslaved to Satan under the Law of Sin and Death (Romans 5:12). Jesus was sent as a ransom to redeem us from bondage (1 Timothy 2:5-6). Since Jesus never sinned, death was powerless over Him and He rose from the dead and conquered death (Acts 2:24). Through repentance and baptism, we can partake in His death and resurrection (Romans 6:2-7); by His shed innocent blood, our sins can be cleansed (1 John 1:9). Therefore, when we die according to the flesh, death will likewise have no power over us and we will resurrect at the last trumpet (1 Corinthians 15).

How do we enter the Kingdom of God? Quite simply, through water baptism and receiving the Holy Spirit (John 3:5). Or it would also be accurate to say that the Kingdom enters *us* (Luke 17:20-21). However, entrance is just the first step—only *inheritance* is permanent. The branches, though they have been grafted into the Vine, will not all remain, except if they bear fruit (John 15:1-10). In the same way, unrighteous saints will certainly not inherit the eternal Kingdom, in spite of having entered through baptism and receiving the Holy Spirit (1 Corinthians 6:9-10, Ephesian 5:5-6, Galatians 5:19-21).

Depending on you Christian background, perhaps these teachings are as foreign to you as they were to me at the time I was first exposed to them. Yet this is exactly what our New Testament teaches, as validated by the AN church. The thesis is this: Christ was sent to redeem us from the Kingdom of darkness, cleanse us, change us, and impart His Spirit in us, such that we can abide in His teachings and bear fruit unto salvation. We are saved by grace through faith. We offer faith; He returns His divine power (grace—see Titus 2:11-14) to change us. Why? "For we are His workmanship, created in Christ Jesus for good works, which God prepared beforehand so that we would walk in them" (Ephesians 2:10).

Maybe a story to illustrate will be helpful here. Let's say you have a motorbike; you start it up, but it won't run. You're not going anywhere! You hire a mechanic and spend a lot of money to make it work. It runs for a short time, but then the same problems recur. You tried your best, and it still doesn't work. What do you do now? You toss the bike!

As un-regenerated people, we are broken and fail to do good. We believe in God to restore us, and by His grace He does it. Now fixed, it's God's intention that we do good. If we fail in this, we are useless to Him and not fixable anymore (Hebrews 6:4-6, Hebrews 10:26-31, 2 Peter 2:20-22). We are, indeed, saved by grace through faith; yet the Scriptures are clear that we are also judged by our works (Matthew 25:31-46 and Matthew 16:27) and by how we have responded to the teachings of our King Jesus (John 12:47-50). That is just the way it is. The whole counsel of Scripture upholds this Kingdom gospel.

This is the gospel of the Kingdom preached by Jesus, the Apostles, and the "appointed and sent" ones (see Luke 10). This was the gospel that Jesus gave Paul on the road to Damascus (Acts 26:16-20). It was the very message Paul was teaching (Acts 28:23, 30-31). This is the revolutionary message that I needed to understand before God would be ready to call me to the mission field, because this is the message that must be preached.

Both in the church and on the mission field, there is an unfortunate emphasis on evangelism—simply preaching the gospel. Yet making converts through preaching alone is not the fulfillment of what we commonly call "The Great Commission." This distinction is paramount to what the Lord was showing me through His Word and through my preparations at this time in my life.

The Great Commission was the mission set forth by Christ for all Christians:

[18] And Jesus came up and spoke to them, saying, "All authority has been given to Me in heaven and on earth. [19] Go therefore and make disciples of all the nations, baptizing them in the name of the Father and the Son and the Holy Spirit, [20] teaching them to observe all that I commanded you; and lo, I am with you always, even to the end of the age." (Matthew 28)

I will excerpt a section from one of my prior booklets below to expand upon what Jesus taught here[4]:

Let's unwrap this a bit, starting with the first word, "go." It does not say "sit and wait," but rather GO! This is not something meant to be confined to the four walls of a building. It does not say to invite folks for Sunday service so they can hear an altar call. It does not say be a nice person and wait for someone to ask you how to be saved. It says GO!

Next, it says what we are to *do*: make disciples. It does not say to get folks to say a magic prayer. It does not say to get people to give you intellectual assent or guilt or fear them into making some sort of profession of "faith." It does not say to invite them to church and hope that years of attendance will slowly lead them to maturity. The marching orders are to *make disciples*. And disciples are defined as those completely surrendered to Christ (Luke 14:25-33) and bearing fruit by obeying Jesus (John 15:8 and 10).

Next it says where to start: baptizing them. No mention of a lengthy baptism class. No waiting for the next scheduled baptism at the local church. The New Testament practice was immediate baptism upon believing and repentance.

Implicit with the command of baptism is repentance and forgiveness of sins. No repentance, no salvation: period. Baptism without repentance is simply taking a bath

---

[4] Excerpted from *Kingdom Expansion Essentials*. Freely available at www.kingdomdriven.org/kingdom-resources.

(see 1 Peter 3:21). Three phrases are used throughout the New Testament that link baptism, repentance, and forgiveness of sins: repentance for forgiveness of sins (Luke 3:3, 24:47, Acts 3:19, 8:22, 11:18), baptism of repentance (Luke 3:3, Acts 13:24, 19:4), and baptism for the forgiveness of sins (Luke 3:3, Acts 2:38). They all go together.

Insist on full repentance. Have them renounce the devil and his works, publicly. Please refer to materials at www.KingdomDriven.org for a deeper understanding of repentance and very effective and simple tools for achieving authentic repentance.

Now, the final command: teach them to obey all Christ's commands. Therefore, our job has just started when we preach the gospel of the Kingdom, take a disciple to surrender and repentance, and then baptize them. Now we have the hard work ahead: teaching them to obey ALL that Jesus commanded. That is the dirty work.

We see in this excerpt what Jesus meant by the Great Commission. It's more than preaching the gospel; it's *making disciples*: baptizing new believers and teaching them to obey all that Jesus commanded. This includes the command to make disciples, doesn't it? Therefore, ALL Christians are called to complete the mission of making disciples. It's a never-ending cycle! Whether at home or on a foreign mission field, in big ways or small, we are *all* invited to participate in the Great Commission and make disciples of our Lord and King, Jesus Christ.

Through my ongoing preparatory period, the Lord showed me how the four phases of mission work were to be implemented. The first phase? Evangelism, followed by discipleship and church development, and (as we will discuss later) culminating in the work of the Great Commandment. With the pieces all in place, God was apparently ready to thrust me into the field. With Kenya on our radar, we now started pressing toward the goal full-speed ahead.

Preparing a family of then ten people to move internationally is not for the faint-hearted. The most important thing I needed was a work permit to obtain a visa to live in Kenya long-term. My host for the short-term trip offered to grant me a work permit; however, as we progressed, I sensed we had conflicting objectives and I slammed the brakes on the process.

Without an alternative way forward, it seemed good to plan a second, exploratory visit to Kenya, where I would touch base with multiple contacts in various parts of the country. The Lord had made it clear that during this visit, He was going to show me where He wanted us to live, and who I would work with.

In preparation for the trip, a friend of a friend gave me a contact in Kenya with whom he had worked for some time. That individual proved very helpful for translating my materials prior to the training missions, and he served as a very capable translator, travelling with me the entire time. On one leg of the mission, I met another man who boasted an existing house church network throughout western Kenya. I learned that the part of the country that both these men were from had a very comfortable climate (due to elevation) and reliable rains; it was also exempt from some of the tribal violence that had been associated with other parts of the country during the recent elections. The Lord gave us clarity: this was the place, and these were the men I would work with to move forward into Kenya.

We immediately started slogging away at the logistical details of the move. With the backing and endorsement from leaders in our house church network, we incorporated a non-profit organization in the US and a Non-Governmental Organization (NGO) in Kenya. The Kenyan organization would be used to grant me a work permit, allowing me legal entry into the country.

At the same time, we leased property (since foreigners can't own land) and began construction of a home in a rural village. Having been unemployed for some time and concentrating on writing, speaking, and exhibiting at homeschool conventions, I now recognized the need for additional income in order to finance the move. I secured a job with a Christian-owned environmental services company. They permitted me to work a four-day work week (to accommodate my speaking schedule on the homeschool convention circuit, as well as the preparations I was making for the shift to foreign missions). In this way, the Lord permitted us to fund the entire transition through our own personal means.

Before I went back to work, at the same time we were trying to sell our home, the Lord spoke to me one morning and told me to buy the house in front of our home…and He said to buy it *that day*! I told Cindy, and then called a brother who was an agent and asked for his help. He said he was busy that day, but I persisted because the message was clear it must be *that day*.

My friend contacted the selling agent and they said it was too late—an offer was already pending. Yet Indiana law requires all offers be presented if no offer has yet been accepted. Our offer led to a bidding war, and we ended up walking away with a 10 year-old, 1,400 square foot home on an acre for just $35,100! Since we accommodated my disabled father on our large homestead, we were a bit perplexed as to how we would house him, along with our large family, in such a small house.

Suddenly, the adjacent house hit the market. We again entered a bidding war, and won the second house for even less than the first one. We moved ourselves and my Dad into both houses within about a month. So there we were, organizing to "sell everything" and move to Africa, and we now owned *three* houses—but not for long! We were able to stage our first house, and it sold within weeks; the profit cleared the balance due on the two new houses. In an amazing move of God, we were now debt-free and owned two houses whose rental income would come to sustain our family's upkeep in the mission field, even to this day.

Prior to our permanent move to Kenya, I was told that we needed to be in-country in person to open the bank account for the NGO and sign some papers for the work permit. I also wanted to inspect the progress of our new family home, as well as do some regional teaching. This time, I brought my oldest son with me to see Kenya for himself, and bring a report back to the family. I knew the importance of gaining consensus for the move among all members of the family. I also knew that in order for the children to make the incredible sacrifices that would be required for this transition, buy-in from a peer (their oldest brother) was vital. Of course, Isaiah fell in love with Kenya and brought the enthusiasm home with him. Now divesting of all their possessions and the comforts of American life was much more palatable to all the children, and we pressed forward with unity and excitement.

The home stretch was getting passports and immunizations, sorting through our possessions, packing our belongings, purchasing flights, and organizing shipment of some of our vital belongings. We also had to have both homes updated and cleaned out for rental. Our 15-passenger van would be sold after it took us to the airport on our final voyage.

Having recently moved from a 3,000 square-foot home with a three-bay garage, to a 1,400 square-foot home without a garage, we had already downsized quite a bit. Now we needed to squeeze all of our belongings into nine totes, nine carry-ons and a 4-by-8 foot crate. Being relatively unattached to possessions myself, this proved easy. We allowed each child to pack their carry-on with what was most important to them. Our final week of packing resulted in filling a 20-foot roll-off with what remained following our "free-cycle" clear-out.

The time finally arrived. We had done everything we could to properly prepare. Before we booked our flight, we were told that our work permit was approved and waiting for us. However, we were suspicious this was not the case when they failed to produce a copy of the approved permit. We pressed forward knowing we would simply get a three-month visitor pass when we arrived at the airport.

The journey was a marathon: three flights with nine large, carry-on bags and eight children over approximately thirty hours. One layover gave us just 45 minutes to catch the connecting flight across the airport. Miraculously, we made it!

Upon arrival, we were greeted by my Kenyan contact with a minivan with no roof rack to carry our nine totes, nine full-sized carry-ons, and twelve passengers. I was skeptical, but somehow we squeezed it all in. Ten hours on terribly rough roads, through the night to our destination, and we made it to our Kenya home!

Of course, we were exhausted after the travel and jetlagged with the time change when we stumbled into our new home at about 4 AM Kenya time. Sifting through our bins, we dug out enough blankets for the children to share on the few beds in the house, and finally managed to get some sleep.

We awoke to absolutely no conveniences whatsoever: no electricity, no running water, no transportation, and nothing to eat except the few items our escort had left us with. Even the bulk of our kitchen items were en-route in the crate, which we didn't know at the time would not arrive until four months later!

So now here I was, with the knowledge, requisite experience, and hopefully the skills necessary to succeed as a pioneer missionary at this totally unknown location. Who would the disciples be? How would I reach them? What would the response be? I had many questions, but also much confidence in God. The four-phase mission was underway, and I was excited to see what would come next.

Chapter 4: The First Phase—Luke 10 Evangelism

After this brief interlude on Luke 10 evangelism, you'll return with me to Kenya, where you'll see it being put into practice on the ground (after some stops and starts, that is). But since Luke 10 is so pivotal to the Kenya mission, and, in fact, any mission field—at home or abroad—it's essential that we look at it before we get much further along. Let's look at the instructive passage for which the "Luke 10 evangelism" method is so aptly named, and then we'll discuss it verse-by-verse:

> Now after this the Lord appointed seventy others, and sent them in pairs ahead of Him to every city and place where He Himself was going to come. [2] And He was saying to them, "The harvest is plentiful, but the laborers are few; therefore beseech the Lord of the harvest to send out laborers into His harvest. [3] Go; behold, I send you out as lambs in the midst of wolves. [4] Carry no money belt, no bag, no shoes; and greet no one on the way. [5] Whatever house you enter, first say, 'Peace be to this house.' [6] If a man of peace is there, your peace will rest on him; but if not, it will return to you. [7] Stay in that house, eating and drinking what they give you; for the laborer is worthy of his wages. Do not keep moving from house to house. [8] Whatever city you enter and they receive you, eat what is set before you; [9] and heal those in it who are sick, and say to them, 'The Kingdom of God has come near to you.' [10] But whatever city you enter and they do not receive you, go out into its streets and say, [11] 'Even the dust of your city which clings to our feet we wipe off in protest against you; yet be sure of this, that the Kingdom of God has come near.' (Luke 10)

Luke 10:1: Now after this the Lord appointed seventy others, and sent them in pairs ahead of Him to every city and place where He Himself was going to come.

It's important to note that this large group of disciples was appointed. To *appoint* is to proclaim one, as to an elected office. (The only other time this word is used in our Bible is when God appointed Matthias to replace Judas in Acts 1:24-25.) In English, we might use the word *ordain*. Therefore, it is accurate to state that Jesus ordained 70 others (that is, in addition to the twelve). In the same way, those sent out in a modern missionary capacity must be set apart and recognized by the church prior to being sent out. The selection of this individual is vital because the first contact people have with the message—and the messenger—will lay the foundation for a new fellowship. Of course, this process of ordaining requires the faith to hear God's voice, for actually, it is He who appoints.

After this large group of evangelists was appointed, they were *sent*. Frankly, the English does not do justice to the word *sent*; or rather, theology does injustice to the Greek word for *sent* and creates a stigma for its proper use. The Greek transliteration for the word *sent* is *apostello*. Do you recognize that word? It is the same root as the word *apostolos* (English *apostle*), which simply means *one sent forth with orders.* Therefore, anyone sent forth with orders, as these 70 were sent by Christ with orders, are apostles. People are fearful of using the word *apostle* today because of the theological connotation. Yet, it is a simple Greek word for *someone being sent with instructions.*

In modern times, we just replace the Greek with Latin and act like that makes all the difference in the world—we use the word *missionary* instead: "the word 'mission' originates from 1598 when the Jesuits sent members abroad, derived from the Latin *missionem* (nom. *missio*), meaning 'act of sending' or *mittere,* meaning 'to send.'"[5]

Today we have replaced *appointed* with ordained, and *apostle* with missionary. Yet, it is still the Lord who calls and sends, by the Holy Spirit and through the agency of the local church. Unfortunately, the advent of denominations and mission agencies has added many layers of bureaucracy to what was once a purely spiritual process.

We see in Acts 13:2-3 how the Lord intended the process to work: "The Holy Spirit said 'Set apart for Me Barnabas and Saul [Paul] for the work to which I called them.'" The church confirmed the calling through prayer, appointed them with the laying on of hands, and sent them. No interview with a sending agency, no years of college training, no required pledges for untold thousands of dollars. Those barriers are all manmade!

Note that Barnabas and Paul were specifically called by God. It was not their own desire or decision to serve God in this way; it was God Himself who had work for which He called them. This is vitally important, especially for foreign missionaries—the pioneer missionaries or "sent ones" that are called to a specific place.

These "international" *sent ones* are different from the indigenous evangelists that are raised up in later phases of a mission. Why the distinction? Although the Scriptures are silent on this point, it may simply be because *foreign service is hard work.* In my short time in the mission field, I have personally seen *eight* families abandon their missions when the going got tough. Of course, people choose to leave for practical or personal reasons—but in these cases, it was in direct response to mission-related difficulties. A clear call and sending from the Lord is essential to perseverance on the mission field.

There is much wisdom in Jesus' instruction for the sent ones to go out in pairs. One of the more practical reasons for this may be security. Two people means an extra set of eyes and ears, as well as an appearance of strength. A second reason for sending two people: twice the discernment in the vitally-important task of identifying the man of peace, whom we will discuss later. Thirdly, all field work is a discipleship opportunity. Therefore, it is wise to send

---

[5] Wikipedia: https://en.wikipedia.org/wiki/Missionary, accessed on 3/221/16.

an experienced person with a learner, if possible. Perhaps most importantly, two people offer mutual accountability. Sending people solo presents temptations in the form of sex, misuse of funds, and even teaching contrary to the Kingdom message. Finally, since these two "sent ones" are sharing the message of the Kingdom, ideally, one person can lead teaching while the other offers prayer support and handles inevitable distractions.

I cannot overemphasize the two-by-two nature of Luke 10 evangelism. Every point in the above paragraph has numerous field examples to back up its importance. Going in pairs doesn't eliminate challenges, but as Ecclesiastes 4:9-10 says, "Two are better than one because they have a good return for their labor. For if either of them falls, the one will lift up his companion. But woe to the one who falls when there is not another to lift him up."

Accountability and securing against temptations are certainly important reasons for the two-by-two rule. We have had many instances where a disciple misrepresents the message or uses the gathering as a means for personal gain. Sending a second person hopefully keeps the message focused on the hard teachings of Jesus, not on the promises of obtaining other benefits.

Many developing nations have a history of white colonials imposing a different law, order, and even culture, usually in exchange for some perceived assistance. Where there is a missionary history, it's often in the form of foreigners coming with a Bible in one hand and a wad of cash in the other. Hospitals, schools, orphanages, care for their neediest, job opportunities, loans…here, these have all been associated with white people *and* missionaries. This certainly can add a level of difficulty to the mission.

I can think of at least five of our house churches that had poor foundations because a disciple went out alone, talked to a bunch of people he knew, and shared a compromised message. In spite of herculean efforts to restore the fellowships, most of the congregants (as contrasted with surrendered disciples), failed to count the cost and latch onto the Kingdom vision. Enter two-by-two. Under the watchful eyes of a partner evangelist, the integrity of the message will remain secure.

In response to this potential problem, our mission instituted common sense rules of engagement for pioneer missions. A first meeting *must* be two-by-two. No disciple launches a mission solo, except for rare exceptions where the evangelist is already tested and ordained by the church. No mention can be made of the mother church, parent mission, *mzungu* (white person), or any offerings of benefits in any way or in any form. As much as it depends on us, the mission is strictly the Word of God.

Luke 10:2: And He was saying to them, "The harvest is plentiful, but the laborers are few; therefore beseech the Lord of the harvest to send out laborers into His harvest.

I'd have to say that the propensity of a *mzungu* to attract all the wrong people has been one of my most perpetual discouragements on the mission field; however, I take comfort in Jesus' own words here. The harvest is plentiful— wow! That takes the pressure off! *The people God has prepared for the Kingdom are ready to hear the message.* Some may complain that "the soil is too hard;" yet, our Lord and King explicitly said *it is harvest time* and the harvest is ready for the picking. We just need to pray that we can discern those whom God has prepared—seek them out, and engage them.

Of course, the harvest is plentiful; but as God does His part in preparing folks, we must do ours in going out and bringing them into the Kingdom. There are few more obvious examples of this cooperative work than one particular day when I was doing a pastoral training mission and we were in the two-by-two evangelism training phase. Two pastors and our field evangelist approached a home and were warmly welcomed by the Mama of the house. Three cups and a hot pot of chai were awaiting them at the table. She told them she was expecting them! The Lord had showed her in a dream the night before that three men of God would visit her that morning to teach her about the Kingdom of God. The pastors were amazed that God had pre-planned their visit! As we go out, we must go in faith, believing that God has prepared those who will receive.

Luke 10:3: Go; behold, I send you out as lambs in the midst of wolves.

Have you ever seen what happens to a sheep in a pack of wolves? Who wants that job? But what that tells us is that a pioneer missionary (or, for that matter, anyone—anywhere—who is sharing the Gospel of the Kingdom and making disciples in accordance with the Great Commission) is foolish to expect that people are going to simply receive the message—or the messenger—with wide open arms. The message of the Kingdom of God is a direct, frontal attack on the Kingdom of darkness. The power of the prince of the air will not simply step aside while you aggressively attack his domain. In fact, Scripture reminds us: "Indeed, all who desire to live godly in Christ Jesus will be persecuted" (2 Timothy 3:12, see also Matthew 5:10-12).

Since we have moved to Africa, I have received multiple death threats, been robbed countless times, suffered a motorbike wreck attributed to witchcraft, had my family threatened, been accosted and ridiculed, been lied to, lied about, swindled, called a devil worshipper, been slandered on a public radio station, had numerous former partners try to send me packing, persevered through two attempted mission coups, been gossiped about and slandered (even by so-called brethren). That's just the way it is. No one who is on the front lines of Kingdom expansion should expect to escape trials and persecution, in one form or another.

Luke 10:4: Carry no money belt, no bag, no shoes; and greet no one on the way.

Here is a controversial topic for our Kenyan disciples: "greet no one on the way." In Kenya, you always greet people; not greeting someone is just plain rude. However, the purpose is simply to remain focused on your primary mission, and to not be deterred from finding your man of peace. Not much more can be said about the latter part of this verse.

The first part of this verse is clear: absent the Word of God, the Spirit of God, and your ministry partner, bring nothing. The reasons for this are self-evident. One is that we are to rely on God alone for the fruitfulness of the mission. Two, we can't engage in the mission with any worldly thing of perceived value, otherwise the prospect will seek the worldly benefit in lieu of the Kingdom message. This is very important to know for first contact in a pioneer field, but it has universal applications.

However, a distinction has to be made here between *open* and *closed* mission fields, because in a closed nation, the Great Commandment work (or some business enterprise) may be the only vehicle by which a missionary can gain entry into the country. In those cases, the alternative effort can simply be used as a front for the foreign missionary to perform undercover gospel work. In open countries, where the gospel can be freely preached, walk empty-handed but full-Spirited.

Ideally the appointed and sent one is to take *nothing* for the journey. However, this seems specific to what we would identify as local, short-term missions (evangelists). The instructions were later modified, perhaps for when the "sent ones" would become international, itinerant workers:

> [35] And He said to them, "When I sent you out without money belt and bag and sandals, you did not lack anything, did you?" They said, *"No*, nothing." [36] And He said to them, "But now, whoever has a money belt is to take it along, likewise also a bag, and whoever has no sword is to sell his coat and buy one." (Luke 24)

Following the dispersion of Christians from Jerusalem, the apostles went out *with* their families and necessities to be able to care for and sustain themselves. History reveals that most of the apostles were married, their wives assisting in the household upkeep. This is implicit in the apostle Paul's question,

> [5] Do we not have a right to take along a believing wife, even as the rest of the apostles and the brothers of the Lord and Cephas? [6] Or do only Barnabas and I not have a right to refrain from working? (1 Corinthians 9)

"Packing a bag" is absolutely necessary today for international travel. You need to make many preparations for legal entry and long-term stay. For an international worker, housing is also a necessity. Though a single worker could realistically stay in other peoples' homes, as recommended in Luke 10, some practical advice is offered in the Wisdom of Sirach in the Septuagint:

> [21] The chief thing for life is water, and bread, and clothing, and an house to cover shame. [22] Better is the life of a poor man in a mean cottage, than delicate fare in another man's house. [23] Be it little or much, hold thee contented, that thou

hear not the reproach of thy house. [24] For it is a miserable life to go from house to house: for where thou art a stranger, thou darest not open thy mouth. (Sirach 29:21-24)

As we had planned and prepared for Kenya, there was much meditation upon, and discussion of, these Scriptures and others. We wanted to make the move in a way that was pleasing to the Lord and in accordance with His Word. So when it came to what to bring, and what to leave behind, and especially where and how we would live, there was often no small debate.

In the matter of housing, we considered proximity to the people we are ministering to, security, size and accommodation (often *necessary* versus *preferred*), long-term plans, and legal considerations. Our goals on the mission field drove the answers to all these questions.

We wanted to launch a mission in the heart of the poor, so we considered both the slums and the village. That question was settled when the Lord ultimately showed us that the village it was. There were no rental properties available that could accommodate our large family, however. (The typical dwelling is the size of an American living room or smaller, and though we were willing to downsize significantly, that was still too much!) We went with the option to build something suitable on a leased property. (If you find yourself in this position on the mission field, I strongly recommend using an attorney for the process because I have seen many people robbed at this phase of establishing their mission.)

Even Paul was self-employed (see 1 Corinthians 9:3-19 and 2 Thessalonians 3:7-9) and rented his own house during his time of house arrest (Acts 28:23, 30-31). He admonished the brethren to work hard so as not to disturb others for assistance (1 Thessalonians 4:11-12). However, it is also clearly expressed that especially itinerant workers (workers who traveled from place to place) were entitled to support (1 Timothy 5:17).

I can reasonably conclude that there is no shame in appointed and sent workers being financially supported. This allows them to commit undivided attention to the Great Commission (2 Timothy 2:4); in fact, foreign governments might prohibit them from generating income, anyway. However, Paul did say that it is better yet *not* to utilize outsiders for support, and rather be self-supported, if possible. This was Paul's boast, and one I have also been blessed to share in.

Our mission, Kingdom Driven Ministries, has been intentionally designed with these teachings in mind. International workers are not supported by the mission; all funding for the mission is utilized for designated earmarks, such as medical missions, the Great Commission, or any other need specifically solicited. None of the international workers have ever received any payment for their services from the mission organization. They are either self-supported or receive financial gifts that are earmarked for them personally. Moving expenses, housing, food, and personal transportation are all self-funded or self-solicited, so that these needs are met without hindering the gospel work, as Paul recommended.

It almost goes without saying that a self-funded missionary or one relying on charitable donations lives by faith. Simplifying one's life to the radical degree that often happens in foreign missions is also a great step of faith. Finally, none of this work is accomplished without faith in a great God doing His part. That's why faith is so essential to embark on a pioneer mission.

Luke 10:5-7: Whatever house you enter, first say, 'Peace *be* to this house.' ⁶ If a man of peace is there, your peace will rest on him; but if not, it will return to you. ⁷ Stay in that house, eating and drinking what they give you; for the laborer is worthy of his wages. Do not keep moving from house to house.

In Luke 10:2, Jesus said that the harvest is ready, even now; yet in the same breath, He says we are sent out as sheep among wolves. How do we reconcile this supposed contradiction? It is only confusing because we fail to recognize that we are not instructed to engage numerous people with broadcast, shotgun-approach evangelism. Instead, we are praying and observing, listening to the Spirit to direct us in a more relational manner to this "man of peace." This process takes discernment.

Gifted evangelists do, indeed, engage crowds. Jesus and Paul taught in the synagogues and other quasi-public places. Peter and John taught in the Temple courts. This method is for those who are gifted and called for such work, for they will certainly face direct persecution (particularly in certain foreign mission locations) and the work may be short-lived. Consider what a pack of wolves would do to a couple sheep standing among them *baa-baaa*-ing away: *Lunch!*

So why did Jesus, and his disciples after Him, engage the crowds, knowing they would face near-certain, mass rejection? We see just one example in Acts 17:1-10. Paul preached to the masses in a public setting; most rejected, but some received the message. They were chased to Berea and the process repeated. This time Paul left strong teachers behind to strengthen the new disciples. We then read in Acts 20:4 that Paul was accompanied by disciples from both Thessalonica and Berea, continuing their discipleship. Therefore, we infer that public evangelism is designed to identify the men of peace who will be engaged in longer-term discipleship.

But for us folks who are not called to be public evangelists, the risk is much lower. We patiently seek direction from the Lord to engage the one, right person. It does not matter if we are ministering to unchurched, cultural Christians, or Muslims. We approach the endeavor with the same method and the same message.

During a pastoral training seminar, I once taught that there is no fear in teaching Muslims (especially in a free country like Kenya). I explained that I had taught and baptized several Muslims. The organizing pastor wanted to see it with his own eyes, and more or less dared me to teach a Muslim when we went out for field evangelism. I asked him, "Do you know where any Muslims live?"

He replied, "No, but there's a mosque here!"

Off we went to the mosque to find a Muslim. Well, we hit the jackpot: the Imam and his family lived next door. I asked if we were welcome to enter his home to teach him about the Kingdom of God. I literally made him verbally ask me to teach it, because I refused to teach in his home without his consent. He said *yes*. I prayed a prayer of peace and taught our *Two Kingdoms* tract. He had some questions and I answered them one by one, never directly insulting Islam or Mohammed. In response to certain inquiries, I used Scriptures to make clear what I believed, or simply said, "You know what I believe about that, why must you hear me say it?" I'll return to this story later.

There are several examples of this Luke 10 evangelism process in the book of Acts; Acts 10:1-11:18 is just one. God had heard Cornelius' (the man of peace) prayers and sent Peter to minister to him. When Peter arrived (I would assume, without greeting anyone on the way) and was welcomed by Cornelius, he found many people assembled. Peter taught them, and they were immediately filled with the Holy Spirit. (This was a unique event for which God had to show the Jews that salvation was open to the Gentiles; normative is for the Spirit to be imparted following baptism.) Cornelius and his household were among those baptized.

Peter and the brethren stayed with them a few days before he returned to Jerusalem. Were the new Gentile believers invited to attend the local church? Nope. There *was* no local church. A church was planted that day, which we can presume continued to meet in the house of Cornelius.

A foreign missionary who chooses to live with the people among whom he ministers has the advantage in finding a man of peace in a grassroots manner. Proximity is also helpful for the process of ongoing discipleship. Pretty much on day one in our little Kenyan village, I met my neighbor, Titus, who owned a small shop across the street. Though I didn't stay in Titus's house, as Luke 10 suggests, he was always around mine, or I visited his little shop. It was a slow process to disciple Titus because he knew very little English, and what he did know was hard for me to decipher. On the other hand, he felt my American English was "hard." With no translator around with the regularity that we visited one another, we just muddled through and made the best of it.

We gave Titus some introductory English learning books, but my Swahili learning had really stalled out due to time constraints once we arrived in Kenya. Thankfully, he picked it up quickly. Eventually, I used a translator to try to teach

Titus, since I could see that he was good-hearted and I hoped he would have a positive response to the gospel of the Kingdom. As we translated more and more resources (such as *The Two Kingdoms* booklet) into Swahili, he was able to learn a lot. Eventually, he surrendered to the Kingdom of God. After a complete year on the mission field, having trained perhaps hundreds and baptized many dozens during pastoral training missions, I remained with just one, single authentic Kingdom disciple. And with that I was very content.

Engaging Titus as my "man of peace" was not quite textbook, but it was certainly God's plan and I recognized it as such. The man of peace is best termed a "person of peace," because *he* can be a *she*. He is someone specifically prepared for your chance encounter with him. He has been seeking God and seeking answers to the big questions. The King and His Kingdom *are* the answers! It usually does not take persuasion and argument to convince the man of peace of the truth regarding the Kingdom of God. When he hears the message, it immediately resonates with him at a deep level. The man of peace is also an influencer and people gravitate to him; he is able to gather a crowd.

Jesus said to stay in his house and DO NOT go house-to-house. Couple this with not greeting anyone along the way and we see that this directly conflicts with classic house-to-house evangelism techniques. Jesus was not after big numbers. If He was, He certainly went about it the wrong way. Let us read what Jesus said to the crowd that followed Him:

> [25] Now large crowds were going along with Him; and He turned and said to them, [26] "If anyone comes to Me, and does not hate his own father and mother and wife and children and brothers and sisters, yes, and even his own life, he cannot be My disciple. [27] Whoever does not carry his own cross and come after Me cannot be My disciple. [28] For which one of you, when he wants to build a tower, does not first sit down and calculate the cost to see if he has enough to complete it? [29] Otherwise, when he has laid a foundation and is not able to finish, all who observe it begin to ridicule him, [30] saying, 'This man began to build and was not able to finish.'... [33] So then, none of you can be My disciple who does not give up all his own possessions." (Luke 14:25-33)

Jesus certainly was not looking to entice people to make a decision by emphasizing the benefits of joining His "movement!" He simply used the crowd as a means of winnowing through them to identify people willing to count the cost, surrender everything, and follow Him unconditionally. Jesus did not want the crowd; He wanted the committed!

Thus, our man of peace is simply the person that the Spirit has already prepared, such that when we present the hard teachings, the high cost, and the total commitment necessary for becoming a Kingdom disciple, they willingly surrender. So why *stay* with the man of peace, as opposed to praising God for the conversion, and moving on?

When the man of peace is identified, we preach the Kingdom, bring him to complete surrender to Christ, take him through repentance, baptize him, and proceed to teach him to obey all that Christ commanded. This is a major time commitment. There is no quick decision and magic prayer and then invite him to church. In fact, in pioneer work, there is often no church to attend. The sent one remains with that disciple and slowly and methodically teaches him and his *oikos* (household).

Focusing on my relationship with Titus and going through the discipleship process was a major effort and a genuine encouragement to me during my first year, as I saw that other methods did not bear the desired fruit. Yet, the fruit of Titus's discipleship was eventually more than evident. The man stepped up and intervened when four men were searching for me to do me bodily harm. He prevented them from advancing by saying, "You want the *mzungu*? *I'm* the *mzungu*! If you want him, you must go through me." I saw him spend the night with a man injured during mob violence who was left for dead. Too late and in too remote of a location to find medical care, Titus sat with him in the street until he died. He also once carried a terribly bloodied patient on his back to a clinic when no one else would go near her.

Our little village is a cesspool of gossip; people live off of it. Yet if people talk against us, Titus always sticks up for us. He helps us in innumerable ways: always willing to interrupt his day to transport someone, pick up something I need, or stand in for a teaching I was supposed to do but can't. When growing new fellowships, there are always heartbreaks and disappointments with various disciples, but Titus has been a rock. I can't count the number of times my family and I have gone through challenging circumstances, and either my wife or I have said, "Thank God for Titus!" Anyone engaging in Luke 10 evangelism (or those who plan to), should not fail to pray, pray, and pray some more to find your man of peace (and ask for discernment to confirm that he is, indeed, the one). You won't be disappointed.

Luke 10:8-9: [8] Whatever city you enter and they receive you, eat what is set before you; [9] and heal those in it who are sick, and say to them, 'The Kingdom of God has come near to you.'

When you stay with the man of peace, you'll eat what they give you. First, I think that's just a sign of respect. I've learned to appreciate, if not enjoy, the chicken gizzard, which is always served to an honored guest. Secondly, it shows, again, that you are reliant upon the man of peace (and God) for your continued provision. This is a minor point, however. The big one is offered in verse 9. What are you to *do* when you find your man of peace? Preach the Kingdom and heal the sick!

Luke 9:2 and 10:9 both record Jesus' command for His appointed and sent ones to heal the sick. This was not an admonition to start a clinic or offer health insurance. Remember, the sent ones had empty bags. This was a command to appeal to Christ in prayer to demonstrate His power so that the people would believe in the message of the Kingdom.

Earlier, I said that I would continue the story of the Imam to whom I preached the Kingdom. When I was done teaching, I asked him if he had any needs that required prayer. He immediately responded that his daughter had been very sick for a long time and he had invested everything he had, but the medical establishment did not help her. I asked for her and he carried her to the room we were in. I laid hands on her and prayed for her healing in the Name of Jesus. At that point, our meeting was over; we shook hands, and I went home.

I came to learn a year later that his daughter had been immediately, permanently, miraculously healed! The Imam surrendered his post in weeks and stopped attending mosque entirely within months. He read and re-read the *Two Kingdoms* tract I had left with him and was convinced the One who had the power to heal his daughter must be the One True God. A year later, he found me through an incredible set of circumstances and he surrendered to Christ, repented, renounced Islam, and is a very strong brother hosting a home fellowship and leading others to Christ to this day. He was a man of peace.

You can see the important role that God's miraculous healing can play in people receiving the Kingdom message. Suffice it to say, Jesus never told us to debate, argue, or convince people into the Kingdom. He told us simply to proclaim the message—the positive message. I really wish I knew that when I was a young Christian. Being zealous and exuberant, and having studied not a little bit in apologetics, I rather enjoyed a good debate. Perhaps there is a place for that, but it is not part of Jesus' instructions for His appointed and sent ones.

Of course, we are always to be prepared to answer the tough questions (see 1 Peter 3:15). Yet this is not necessarily confrontational. Answering heartfelt questions and addressing common objections is part of the task. However, discern the underlying spirit of the interaction: is it sincere, or is it adversarial? Is it designed to discredit the message or undermine the messenger? Stick to the positive message, encouraging the listeners to save their questions until you finish sharing the Kingdom with them. Never lead with the negative, i.e., discrediting or undermining their beliefs. Simply teach the Kingdom gospel and wait and see if the message reaches their heart. If it does, the mind will catch up later.

As you share the Kingdom Gospel, don't teach assertively what you do not know for certain. A sincere person knows that no human knows everything. If there are questions for which you do not have a ready answer, tell the prospect you will get back to them, and try to do so after some study. If you answer falsely just to try to look good, and the prospect recognizes it, you will jeopardize your credibility and therefore the credibility of the Word you represent. It is always better to be honest. If the prospect is good-hearted, they want the truth, not easy answers—so they will be patient and wait.

Luke 10:10-11: [10] But whatever city you enter and they do not receive you, go out into its streets and say, [11] 'Even the dust of your city which clings to our feet we wipe off *in protest* against you; yet be sure of this, that the Kingdom of God has come near.'

With Luke 10 evangelism, we can expect positive results, because Jesus said the harvest is ready. But we are not instructed to do battle with the wolves. Therefore, if a good-hearted man of peace does not welcome you, Jesus simply says to dust off your feet and move on.

This last step of Luke 10, wiping the dust from your feet if necessary, requires just as much faith as any other step in the process. It can be hard to know when to persevere in looking for a man of peace and when to move on; discerning and trusting God's leading is essential.

I remember once, I baptized a former Muslim teacher at a Madrassa, along with his wife, other family members, and numerous people from his community. It looked like a very promising situation. However, not too much time passed before I discovered he was still smoking cigarettes, which he refused to acknowledge as a problem. Then, others in the community revealed that he was a practicing witchdoctor. If that were not enough, some who left the fellowship said that the man had gotten a crowd to come hear the teachings by promising them benefits; in fact, he presented himself as a bishop who worked with many *wazungu* (white people). In the end, he asked me for a loan to start a business (since he had to leave his job at the Madrassa). He misused most of the money and never repaid any of it.

I discreetly tried to discern if any of the disciples that had been identified through this fraudulent "man of peace" were men of peace themselves, or if anyone had genuinely repented in response to the Kingdom message. In time, it became obvious that the entire fellowship had simply been built on the wrong foundation. I was left with no choice but to wipe the dust off my feet and move on.

The topic of Luke 10, as you can see, has many nuances that one does not immediately discern upon a cursory reading of the Scriptures. Yet this understanding is foundational to the success of a pioneer mission, such as we were about to embark on. The job of a "sent one," or pioneer missionary, sent to a foreign mission field is to develop a sustainable, reproducible mission. It starts with the first phase of evangelism, which prepares you for what comes next. In the case of a pioneer foreign mission, God's prescription (gleaned from Scripture) is to start with Luke 10 evangelism.

Chapter 5: False Starts and Frustrations

Before long, we made the brick "barn" on under half an acre our home. However, the honeymoon did not last long. Within a week we learned some bad news: a Kenyan we had trusted stole a large sum of money from us, money we had set aside to eventually purchase a car. We were devastated. It was the first taste of betrayal we had experienced on the mission field.

Meanwhile, we had not received our work permit yet. This was a real concern. In spite of several long trips to Nairobi, upon assurances that it was ready and I just needed to pick it up, we were without legal status to work in Kenya. We never were able to determine the source of the hang-up with the work permit, but the difficulties certainly put a damper on our enthusiasm in getting started on the mission.

A couple of months after our arrival, we enjoyed a short time of teaching, evangelism, and fellowship with a group of four short-termers from America. During the evangelism mission, we were accompanied by my neighbor Titus, whom I have already shared was my "man of peace."

I had done my share of short-term missions, and now had the opportunity to host some brothers and try to find a place for them in our albeit fledgling mission. Having gone through this cycle many times now, and also having talked to many other missionaries who have had visitors intent on serving, I think this is a good place to interject just a few thoughts on welcoming short-term missionaries.

On the positive side, missionary tourists usually bring back awareness of the realities (and needs) in an impoverished nation to many others who might not otherwise understand. They often become spokespeople and advocates for particular causes that have impacted them from abroad. They may acquire a lifelong commitment to support foreign missions, or become inspired to be involved in longer-term missions themselves (ironically, three out of four of our early visitors went on to become full-time missionaries!). Finally, they almost certainly gain an awareness of the huge disparity between Western lives and the lives of those in a developing country.

Also on the positive, these short-termers bring excitement to the indigenous churches, lending credibility to the Kingdom cause by showing locals the global nature of the Kingdom. Perhaps the greatest positive effect we have seen in short-term missionaries visiting an apostolic mission is that they receive real field training on concepts and methods for which stateside, qualified trainers are in short supply. Our mission has sent many people home with knowledge and tools, and an unquenchable exuberance, which has spread like a wildfire in their sphere, resulting in mobilization of the saints on the home front—*not* on the foreign mission field.

Culturally, people in developing nations appreciate and honor visitors, especially if they come from far away. I think Western brethren visiting fellowships in developing nations can be encouraging to all parties. However, if visitors come in with unrecognized biases or personal agendas, these can be obvious to the indigenous brethren and can create problems with the mission's ongoing work. In general, potential problems of all kinds can be avoided if short-termers come in with respect for the existing mission and understand the potential impact of some of their actions.

It behooves all short-term missionaries and other visitors to understand the mission they will be visiting, the culture, the indigenous disciples, and other significant dynamics of the mission. Following the suggestions and cooperating with the goals of the mission leadership is a vital component of a successful short-term mission. Remember, they will soon be gone and others will be left behind to carry things forward.

Concerning the types of short-term visitors, there are several. We have already mentioned those coming to be trained and mobilized. That is the most worthwhile and fruitful short-term mission, in my opinion. There are those who want to simply see the developing world with their own eyes. This can be a life-changing event and instill a lifetime commitment to support the neediest in the world. This can also be fruitful. A third is donors, who want to get to know the people and programs they've invested in, and validate their ongoing support. This is obligatory, and can help or hurt the mission, depending on if the supporter and the mission leadership are ideologically "on the same page."

One other type of visitor comes with the goal of being involved in the "Great Commission" work: evangelism, preaching, or teaching. This type of visit, and its outcomes, needs to be honestly assessed. First of all, if the person is not doing these things stateside, it is not necessarily safe to assume that God is calling them to do it in a foreign location. The mission field is really not the place to "practice." A poor delivery by a Westerner can create difficulties of various kinds for long-term missionaries. Specifically, false teachings or a bad Christian example will be hard to undo because being a *mzungu* and being from far gives instant, yet underserved, credibility to the message. Yet doing field work, under the tutelage of a tenured field guy, can be a great opportunity to help a less-experienced evangelist master the craft.

With visits such as this, I think the objective should be discipleship for the visitor, not conversion for the indigenous people. Therefore, all teaching and evangelism should be done in partnership with a long-term missionary; after all, his team will be responsible for any ongoing discipleship that results from the visit. No lasting fruit will be borne without this cooperation.

What about short-term missionaries doing service projects? Service is something we are commanded to do as Christians. It is only logical to want to direct that service towards the neediest people in the world, right? Well, *yes* and no. If you have a talent that the local population does not have, it makes sense. However, to do projects for which local talent is available (with funding being the only limitation) is of questionable wisdom. Flights alone cost much, much more money than many of the projects completed during short-term trips. It would, therefore, be a better use of resources to allow long-term missionaries already on the ground to organize such projects using indigenous workers. Poverty is typically a result of a lack of employment opportunities, not a shortage of laborers; executed with this in mind, projects can boost the poor while maintaining their dignity by giving them needed work.

I would suggest that it is better yet to train locals in whatever skills may be lacking to bring a project to completion—the whole "teach a man to fish" thing. It's worthy to note that many Westerners visit Africa in hopes of assisting with various skills, such as construction\ or other trades. While I lived stateside, I thought such visits of noble intent would only be a benefit to a developing nation. Having lived here for some time now, I realize that African ways of doing these things are, by necessity, so different from the "American way," that it is better to let indigenous people do the work the way they find best, and if they need training, to have it done at the hands of a local mentor. An unintended outcome of providing free training is the negative impact it has on a vital industry here— the existing schools and training facilities. Free labor can actually undermine an African's job. Thus, a short-term missionary should come with the overall goal of imparting unique skills that will have a verifiable benefit and not inadvertently hurt anyone. For example, medical and dental clinics, business seminars, agricultural training, and such specialized endeavors, can prove very beneficial to the local populations.

As you can see, the impact left by short-term missions can be, overall, either positive or negative. A thorough assessment and conversation about goals and plans for the visit is vital, and the visitors must respect the ongoing work of the mission enough to heed advice and work in cooperation with mission staff and indigenous brethren.

During that first short-term visit by my American brothers, we focused largely on evangelism, as well as just introducing them to life in a developing nation. Unfortunately, the visit was somewhat tainted by my Kenyan friend bringing further work permit issues to the forefront. After the Americans left, I rushed to Nairobi yet again, to intervene in the permit process with a new advocate. We prayed much at that time for the Lord's intervention. In my absence, the rogue brother was now overtly threatening to forcefully expel my family from the village. The Lord answered my prayers with a Word: *persevere, and trust in Him.*

I felt that this was all happening because, while in Nairobi, I was working with another brother to prepare our first field evangelism tract. I had been percolating ideas all the while my American brothers had been visiting, as we reached out with the Kingdom message in our village community. I was sure Satan was trying to stop the process. I felt God say, "nothing is as it seems, and everything will be fine." I was immediately at peace and pressed on with the plan of writing and illustrating the booklet. In a short time, not only was it completed, but the work permit was finally approved. To God be the glory!

If a work permit is required in your situation, I urge you to proceed with caution in selecting with whom you apply for that permit. When it comes to this issue of work permits, where they are required, a mission can end as quickly as it began. If you find yourself in this situation, my advice is only to work with indigenous people that have been time-tested and proven faithful by people you trust. This doesn't apply to all readers (or all missionary locations), of course, but I felt compelled to include it for those "sent ones" who are reading for information and advice.

Once I was legally permitted to work in Kenya, I got serious on the mission. I had already done extensive training during my previous three short-term trips, and even made numerous contacts during our multi-village foray when the Americans visited. In fact, I had a backlog of invitations for multi-day training missions. We would train for a day or two on the message and the mission, and then go out in the field in small teams, preaching the Kingdom gospel. We would then take surrendered folks through repentance and baptize them. Because these meetings were always hosted in a church by a local pastor, these new disciples were, by necessity, relinquished to the pastors for ongoing discipleship.

Though I believed in the Luke 10 method of evangelism as the biblical ideal, I persevered with these meetings for some time in an attempt to mobilize local ministers in these practices. The teachings were not watered down in the least and people responded very positively to the message, mission, and methods for effective Kingdom expansion. As an added benefit of the process of teaching these various church groups, I was also thoroughly discipling my field team and translators.

Over time, several pastors, leaders, and church members professed agreement with Kingdom teachings, and even expressed interest in adopting New Testament practice of house church. Ultimately, however, little to no fruit ever materialized from these field efforts. I was deeply concerned that the newly-baptized saints were not properly discipled in the traditional church environment; any seeds that were planted seemed quickly uprooted.

One of the things I had learned during my career as a project manager was the necessity of iterative evaluation and change. One can't press forward with a plan toward a goal and never make changes to that plan. Certainly, this valuable management mindset was a gift from the Lord as I sorted out how the pioneer missionary ought to implement this mission! I guess you could say I was trying to press forward with evangelism, but found that neither the disciples nor was I happy with the outcome. As a result, at some point, my strategy shifted slightly in an attempt to correct some obvious issues.

I saw that if the host pastor did not embrace the Kingdom teachings, but some of the church members did, there would be conflict. He would feel a threat to his leadership, and the congregants would either leave the church or have to return to the denominational fare. I decided that it was best to engage only the pastors, not members who were also interested in the teachings. In this way, the pastors who accepted the teachings could present them to the congregations at the proper pace, through personal discipleship.

In the end, I don't think one pastor honestly subscribed to the teachings of the Kingdom, although many said they did. And, most meetings continued to include church congregants, in spite of my urging them not to. In time I saw that the conversion to Kingdom teachings and the discipleship that I hoped to see were not manifesting in the institutional environment. Eventually, I abandoned pastoral training altogether and persevered in doing grassroots evangelism and discipleship in the villages—classic "Luke 10."

I thought that equipping Kenyan Church leadership on Kingdom expansion best-practices might be beneficial. After all, Kenya is a post-Christian environment and folks were pretty well familiar with some aspects of Christianity and with the expectation of attending church. Thus, we also started a home fellowship in our village with several of our neighbors. Unfortunately, since the basis was not a "man of peace," we experienced difficulties from the get-go.

I think it would be instructive at this point to share just a few observations on the difference between pre-Christian and post-Christian mission fields, as each one will come with a different set of expectations and perhaps different strategies. Some of this has been gleaned (the hard way) from my experiences in Kenya.

The Insanity of Obedience by Nik Ripken challenges those interested in foreign missions to consider the work that God is doing, and participate in it. The author makes a distinction between "Pre-Pentecost," "Pentecost," and "Post-Pentecost" environments. However you describe it, the question is: *has Jesus been known in the area in which you want to minister?* Can the typical missionary methods be used there? Is it an area where believers will be persecuted, and if so, how will you prepare them for that reality? Many other questions emerge, but Ripken focuses his work on areas where there are Hindu- or Muslim-Background Believers, rather than post-Christian areas such as Kenya where some version of the gospel is familiar.

Pioneering new ground on a fresh foundation was the apostle Paul's objective, so as not to interfere with other men's work: "And thus I aspired to preach the gospel, not where Christ was *already* named, so that I would not build on another man's foundation" (Romans 15:20). This is a noble goal, and a pioneer missionary may utilize some of the same methods as those described in this book, but there are special considerations which may need to be made.

In a pre-Christian or unchurched environment, much more emphasis will be given to the foundational stories of the Bible concerning Creation, man's fall, God's interactions with the Old Testament saints, and the Person and work of Christ. Since these events are presumed to be understood by New Testament readers, the Kingdom message we preach (using *The Two Kingdoms*, for example) relies on a certain basic foundation.

Teaching in an unreached environment is a breath of fresh air, because a "blank slate" can receive the Kingdom message in its intended simplicity. In my experience, it has been much easier to disciple converts from among the unchurched, or even other religions, than to restore cultural Christians to Kingdom practice. The unlearning necessary to truly surrender to Christ and His teachings is hard for many to accept.

Our second mission front in Uganda was purposely selected in a nearly-unchurched area. There are a few churches, yet such a vast majority of the population has never entered one, that it is almost virgin territory. In fact, never has anyone we have encountered seen a Bible in their language. As a result, we have not had to deal with an institutional church environment or competing doctrines. In fact, the best day to teach in this area is on Sunday; culturally, Ugandans take Sunday off work, but few in this particular area attend church. Therefore, we have found our disciples very easy to organize for Sunday meetings. What a blessing it has been.

That brings us to considering the post-Christian environment. Our mission in Kenya is certainly categorized as post-Christian, as are most Western nations. With approximately 80% of the population of Kenya considered "Christian" and only a small fraction of them reportedly attending church, the stats paint a dismal picture. Many calling themselves "Christian" are really just identifying themselves as "non-Muslim." Those involved in churches can be corrupted by a gospel of easy-believism or by the prosperity gospel (which is, of course, very attractive).

Regardless of the location or the people group, a good rule of thumb is to *approach every prospect as if they need a fresh start.* Out of all of our members in our numerous churches, only three people have not required renewed repentance and an authentic baptism, or rebaptism, as it were. For most, the Kingdom of God represents a radical departure from cultural Christianity.

Any differences between the various Christian denominations and even Muslims center around one core issue: *what do they do with Jesus and His teachings?* Doctrinally, this is our major area of no-compromise. Muslims believe that Jesus is simply one in a line of prophets; cultural Christians essentially believe He is a Savior and the means by which we enter heaven through faith. We believe, as I previously mentioned, the gospel of the Kingdom: that Jesus is the King, sent to redeem us from Satan, sin and the world; to restore us as children of God and citizens of His Kingdom; and to equip us to walk in love and obedience. Failure to change our ways means we will fail to inherit the Kingdom we have entered (or rather, which has entered us). This is the foundation of Christ's teachings, in harmony with all the epistles and the witness of the early church. It takes a whole lot of mental and theological gymnastics to get around the fact that Jesus' teachings were meant to be followed.

The alternative is truly unfathomable: that Jesus was just kidding about everything He said, or that He literally taught hard things just to show us what we could never achieve. Well, the apostolic (New Testament) church and the Ante-Nicene church lived, suffered, and many were martyred for the privilege of upholding the literal teachings of Jesus. Study their witness for yourself with an open mind if you think otherwise.

As you can see from my story thus far, I worked hard to partner with indigenous pastors in many ways. I presented these multi-day pastoral training seminars all over Kenya in an attempt to reach the local pastors with the Kingdom gospel and organic Kingdom expansion practices. The teachings were always well received; that is, as long as we went home when we were done and did not plant a fellowship in their back yard.

Thus, as I said, we actually started our own home fellowship, which at first was really just opening our home and seeing who would come. And come, they did. However, in time we learned that in spite of verbal assent to all the teachings of the Kingdom, nearly all of these church attendees would be caught in various sins: prostitution, abortion, extramarital relations, theft, deceit....you name it. As well, many of them also asked for a "loan" (typically for a small business) and defaulted on it, never returning to the fellowship. Without the Kingdom in their hearts, of course those who came to our fellowship did not live exemplary lives between Sunday services. And when everyone *but* you knows the character of those you walk with, the folks who might be genuinely interested in the message unfortunately keep their distance.

Although we were looking to experience true house church, in the sense of assembling as a *called out* people, we began by attracting a never-ending cycle of visitors rather than committed members with interest in the Kingdom message. Of course, here in Kenya, people *love* visitors—especially in church!

At this point, the influx of visitors was more of a distraction. As we will discuss later, with our second attempt at home fellowship with actual *called out* brethren, we did our best to take advantage of the frequent visitors as another means of Kingdom expansion. Our focus became, then, to convert people from visitors to Kingdom disciples—from *friends* to *brothers*. Thus, immediately after fellowship, visitors are invited to stay for teachings after everyone else leaves, and they are presented the gospel of the Kingdom. Sometimes, they are taught through to baptism that day, but most of the time the teaching is organized in two sessions.

Through many false starts and frustrations my first year, I was learning and making adjustments as necessary. It was time to get rid of all the "fluff" and get back to the basic recipe: Luke 10 evangelism. With this in place, the mission jumped into high gear; we were able to shift our focus from evangelism to the next two phases of the pioneer mission: discipleship and church development.

Chapter 6: Discipleship—the Dirty Work

Obviously, my early experiences on the mission field—focused on working in churches and with pastors—were proving fruitless. God was showing me how very important it was, and why, to implement this Luke 10 method on the mission field. The first phase of the pioneer mission is evangelism, and the message is the gospel of the Kingdom. The best presentation of that particular message is the Luke 10 method that Jesus used with his own disciples when He sent them out.

Although we are not all "sent ones" in the sense of being called to a specific place, we all are told to "go and make disciples" (see Matthew 28:19-20). This method of sharing the message that God gives us should not be ignored. Though the world and even the church will use different methods, it always pays to obey God's Word. It may not be obvious to us *why* (especially in terms of numbers or visible outcomes), but we should still strive to do what He said. As my personal journey unfolds, you'll now see the two-by-two and other elements of Luke 10 come alive.

A highlight during our first year (needful because of so many discouragements) was a visit from Glenn Roseberry (now a dear brother and partner in the mission). He visited us in Kenya, though his final destination was Tanzania. At that time, I was still organizing weekly or even twice-weekly pastoral training missions. We modeled the Luke 10 method by taking the pastors and participants out into the field two-by-two to share the gospel using *The Two Kingdoms*. Glenn immediately latched on to the biblical method of preaching the Kingdom, making disciples, and organizing home fellowships. After a few weeks of training, Glenn (a pioneer missionary himself) moved on to the location of his calling, with the goal of developing his own sustainable reproducible mission! I am happy to report that his work is bearing fruit for the Kingdom as he, also, has slowly and steadily implemented the Luke 10 mission model in various places.

I mentioned that just prior to going to Nairobi to finally get my work permit, I and some American brothers went out into the village two-by-two. I knew it was important to use this method in my own village; however, the "Achilles' heel" in this case was the fact that we were a bunch of *wazungu*. The exception was Titus, our neighbor and my first disciple in Kenya. Many, many times have I praised God for Titus; he is truly my "man of peace" and a dearly loved brother. Of course, you've already read about him a bit, but it's worth repeating just how much of an encouragement he was to me during our first year in Kenya.

With some false starts during my first year, and with lots of learning from experience under my belt, I resolved to move ahead making those iterative changes I mentioned earlier. I was excited! Titus became an invaluable help in vetting future, prospective disciples. He was a gatekeeper of sorts; while his discernment was sometimes off, the deck was slowly being re-stacked more in our favor.

Titus began to autonomously share the Kingdom message with people and engaged in some beginning discipleship with them, independent of me. He was able to identify people who were interested in the message rather than the *mzungu*. Of course, there were still occasional problems because we live in a small village and everyone knew of our relationship. Even so, this was a great leap forward in the spread of the Kingdom in my corner of Kenya.

After the complete failure of our first attempt at home fellowship in our village, we shut it down and began focusing on these Luke 10 missions, which typically began as visits with contacts from my previous pastoral training meetings. However, I was still the primary evangelist and teacher; therefore, I continued to attract a disproportionate number of people with motives other than the Kingdom of God. Yet even in compromised house churches, some Kingdom brethren did emerge—men of peace, per se.

We started one home fellowship centered around a pastor we will call Linus, right outside a city not far from our home. Remember the failed fellowship surrounding the former Muslim Madrassa teacher and witchdoctor? Well, Linus was introduced to me by a former member of that group.

At that time, I had agreed to teach a full-semester Kingdom Discipleship course at a local Bible college. Linus and his wife were among the attendees. They were very personable and expressed interest in starting up a fellowship at their home. We began to visit Linus' village and preach the Kingdom message. We baptized over a dozen people there: older men, women, and youth (that is, under 35 years). It seemed a very promising fellowship and continued on for several months, though not quite a year. That is when I received the call.

Linus' wife called and told me Linus had taken another woman to be his wife—another church member who just so happened to be married with numerous children herself. Oh dear! I immediately organized with a couple of our leaders to visit their home and get to the bottom of the crisis. There was no denying it: Linus had done just what his wife had claimed. And come to find out, she was actually his *fourth* wife! He had been deceiving everyone all along.

One of the issues prompting the disagreement between Linus and his wife was misuse of money that was meant to assist the local needy. There was also some issue with another brother, Timothy, who had been asked to secure a scholarship for the son of Linus' wife. We called upon Timothy to see what was going on in this very confusing situation.

It turns out Timothy had left the fellowship months back, due to the known duplicity of Linus. Timothy shared openly with us (with Linus and his wife present), the affairs that had transpired there. It was a sordid ordeal, to say the least. The entire fellowship was an act of deception, Linus having promised a school, a hospital, and other benefits in exchange for the congregants' support for him as leader of this new fellowship. As the congregation learned that Linus' promises were empty, many people were leaving.

In the end, Linus and his new "wife" were unwilling to cease their relationship and Linus was informed that by his decision, he was officially put out of the church. It was not received well; he literally chased me with a machete! Praise the Lord, I escaped unharmed.

Despite this unfortunate turn of events, I was happy to open up dialogue with Timothy, whom I had known was a sincere brother from the very first day. He supported his own family by his own means, and even cared for his aged father. He was a very talented football (soccer) coach who volunteered his time to keep youth off the street and prepare them to compete competitively. He was formerly a karate instructor and very active in politics. But when he was exposed to the Kingdom, he abandoned all these worldly pursuits and devoted his efforts to expanding the Kingdom of God. I remember him coming to me with many questions and some confusion, not knowing how to make the changes he desired in his life because people just kept calling him and distracting him. Finally, in desperation, he simply removed the SIM card from his phone and cut it up! In the end, Timothy was a real man of peace.

As you can see, my first and even second years were filled with a lot of activity that ended up not being very fruitful; in contrast, the slow-and-steady discipleship with Titus would be more profitable than I expected. Yet even the pastoral training served its purposes in identifying men of peace, like Timothy, who had a genuine interest in the Kingdom.

The work was often exhausting and demoralizing. I was emotionally drained. The constant betrayals, in particular, really interfered with our ability to develop the trust necessary to nurture and enjoy authentic fellowship. Even so, we continued to pour ourselves into the disciples, worked hard to assume the best, and oftentimes suffered more and more heartache as three in four of them ultimately went away from the truth. But it was the one in four authentic brethren, as well as the grace of God, that kept us energized to press on.

As the one-in-four became several disciples, the mission started to take shape. By the end of the second year, we had re-launched a home fellowship with dozens of genuine disciples and many seekers. We also had multiple fellowships birthed in other villages (including Timothy's), most of which remain strong to this day. At this point, I had completely stopped doing pastoral training missions.

We experienced a burst of growth among an important village demographic that would ultimately have a serious impact on the future of the mission. The message of the Kingdom was attracting *wazee* (old men). This is significant because in Kenyan culture, the elders are revered and their wisdom respected by the youth (which is anyone under the age of 35). By the end of our third year in the field we had taught and baptized a dozen *wazee*, which resulted in over a dozen more joining in later months.

As our *wazee* have matured, they have been an example in our community. They often visit satellite fellowships as a show of solidarity and support, which speaks influence into those communities and helps the fledgling churches to grow. Perhaps most importantly, we have begun to exercise both biblical church leadership and church discipline in ways which were difficult with our previous demographics.

Early on in the mission, I was focusing on the first phase of the sustainable reproducible mission process—evangelism. During the latter part of my second year, I was able to shift to the second phase, discipleship, in concert with church development. Discipleship is a hands-on activity. It is the hard stuff and, indeed, the dirty work. Let's take a look at teaching, modeling, and counseling—all of which I consider essential elements of discipleship.

Teaching is simply providing a sufficient knowledge foundation to equip a disciple for decision-making and life change. (Of course, change only happens by the power of the Holy Spirit, but we need knowledge of *what* to change.) Acquiring that foundation involves Bible study, reading books, attending training sessions, participating in small groups, and doing one-on-one teaching.

The *modeling* aspect of discipleship happens when a mentor is able to show a disciple how to apply the Scriptures; this occurs in the process of doing life together. The disciples here have closely monitored how I live my life; gossip throughout the village upon every turn of events bears this out with consistency. How I respond to challenges is particularly under a microscope. Truthfully, the test has not been what I have exhibited during mountain-top experiences, but rather how I have endured during hardships.

During my second year in Kenya, I was in a serious motorcycle accident. I was on my way to a mission with a translator and was forced off the road at about 70 kph, down an abrupt drop-off. It was reported that the bike rolled three times as we were thrown from the bike. I recall in somewhat of a daze standing up immediately to check if my translator was alright. Three men lifted the bike off of him; he said he was fine and I immediately went unconscious.

Next thing I knew, I was being carried to a passing car that had been flagged down to serve as my ambulance. They tried to put me in the front seat, but I told them I could not bend my right knee. They put me in the backseat. I was completely incoherent because of the shock, but at a critical intersection I told them the name of a hospital I wanted to go to. This forced them to go to a different hospital in a more distant city, but I thank God, because it likely saved my leg.

As the 1.5 hour trip progressed, my wits returned and I now knew what was going on. At the hospital they tried to remove my pants to see my leg. I insisted they cut the pants off; then we all saw the damage. My flesh was torn open in a swath about five inches wide on my knee. All the soft tissue was pulled up as a flap and my bones were visible. This was a surprise to everyone, because never did a drop of blood hit the ground—that is, until they exposed it.

When they inspected the wound and cleaned it, it was more pain than I had ever experienced. Yet the entire time I never ceased praising God, praying, and even singing. My translator, who was still accompanying me, and the medical staff were amazed. An exposed ligament was 50% torn. Surgery was recommended, but it was so painful I told them to close it up; it would have to heal on its own.

While the doctor was stitching me, I prayed in earnest, because he only gave me a dozen or so shots of local anesthetic; however, these went through the dangling flap of flesh but not into the lower flesh. That meant when the doctor installed the oh-so-many stitches, each time that long curved needle did its arc to connect the half inch thick flap to the muscle below, it was in exposed muscle tissue that had received no anesthetic whatsoever. OUCH! But I kept praying and praising God.

The Lord had showed me before the wreck that He really wanted me to work on a writing project. However, I was doing one or two missions weekly, rendering me way too busy to get to it. Ironically, He slowed me down! Without being able to walk or ride, I was bedridden. I finished the project in exactly twenty days. It always pays to be attentive to the Lord's voice. When I received the flood of visitors over the next couple months, I shared with them that the downtime allowed me to work on something the Lord deemed more important. Therefore, I was praising God for the injury.

As well, during this event, the Lord revealed to me that I would be back on my bike in three weeks. At the time, we had still not done an x-ray because they wanted to stitch me up to stop the bleeding first. And the condition of my motorcycle was completely unknown. Yet I posted on Facebook (and shared with the disciples) that I would be back on the mission in three weeks. And what happened? In exactly three weeks to the day, I drove my bike solo and taught a three day pastoral training mission. Many in our fellowship took great encouragement from this testimony and it served as an important reminder of the importance of listening to the Lord and suffering trials with grace.

Indeed, my disciples watch me—both the good and the bad. Here is a *bad* example from the trenches. The challenges of leading both an NGO and a mission while living among an impoverished people with certain cultural expectations will undoubtedly create frustrations, which can easily be made evident through body language, words, or even occasional outbursts. Likewise, a vision-bearer and a shepherd of that vision will undoubtedly interact with other workers who have a contrary vision. In either case, the result is *conflict*.

Though I will always apologize and even publicly confess and repent if my behavior amounted to sin, my impromptu responses to challenges have proven very detrimental to the mission on occasion. The expectations of a foreign missions leader have been an impossible standard to live up to, and the Lord constantly reminds me of my humanity. However, I do appreciate the advice and encouragement of my brother Titus, who has said, "When you lead many people and everyone, they come to you, it's a must to get angry sometimes." I definitely appreciate that grace when it is extended, but unfortunately, sometimes it is lacking for one in leadership.

The last of the three key elements of discipleship is *counseling*, which is usually also a part of doing life together. I would argue that there is little basis for counseling apart from authentic relationship. That fact has created a huge challenge for our foreign mission because of what we call the *"mzungu* factor." The *mzungu* factor is the phenomenon of how people think of and respond to white people. Because of Kenya's colonial history and the first waves of missionary activity, white people are typically looked upon as *wazungu* and not just other brethren. It takes a lot of patience and persistence to break through that particular barrier. Add language and culture differences and the problem is magnified further.

The ideal scenario is to break through to the first generation of disciples, filtering through the many to get through to the few, and allow those disciples to forge the authentic relationships necessary to facilitate true discipleship. Bear in mind, the objectives of sustainability and reproducibility necessitate passing the discipleship baton, anyway.

Recently, Timothy (whose story you just read) discovered that his wife was deceiving him and undermining a major family decision he had made. He felt terribly betrayed. He thought it was hopeless and wanted to just let her go away. I took the time to counsel him about leadership in the home, developing consensus with his wife and children, not winning battles to lose the war, Satan's program to destroy his marriage and his children's faith, and loving her by way of example. He went home and apologized to his wife and older boy and relationships began to be restored. Just four weeks later, one of his disciples experienced a nearly identical situation with *his* wife. My brother, in turn, counseled his disciple in the same way that I had done with him. With much drama, prayers, and fanfare, his disciples' marriage was also restored. Timothy said, "I believe that God allowed me to go through that so I could minister to my brother in the same situation!"

As you can see, the elements of modeling and counseling are active and occur in the context of real-life situations. The teaching aspect can also be integrated in this manner, but it is often relegated to a classroom setting. As

Westerners, we are more intellectually-driven, and most of us probably grow in our faith through reading and learning. Here on the mission field, we also rely on printed materials to lay a strong foundation, and because of the number of our disciples, I do teach classes. However, teaching as the primary means of discipleship is not adequate in and of itself.

Especially in developing nations, where there is an oral tradition and so many still are not literate, relying on classroom teaching as a means of evangelism and discipleship will create a one-generation mission, not a reproducing movement of the Kingdom of God. As well, we cannot expect folks in other cultures to view the Scriptures and its stories in the same manner that we, as Westerners, do.

When it comes to discipleship, I have found that the modeling and counseling components are key to building strong followers of Christ (particularly in other cultures). The "teachable moments" of everyday must be leveraged for their growth. Many times, I've thought that this person or that person just "didn't get it," only to have them experience a real "Aha!" moment when I or someone else was able to guide and teach them through a real-life challenge or temptation. Discipleship is hands-on, and we must look for consistent ways of bringing Jesus into people's everyday experience. It takes patience and time, especially for us Westerners, who often want instant results.

I would go so far as to say that some people actually will not experience Christ and own the teachings of the Kingdom until they mess up and someone leverages that experience for their discipleship. It's like the apostle Peter, who sat and listened to Jesus' teachings in the Sermon on the Mount and the Sermon on the Plain: love your enemies, blessed are the peacemakers—but when Jesus was threatened in the Garden of Gethsemane, Peter still pulled out his sword and cut off the ear of the High Priest's servant. When corrected by his master, we see that he did not repeat this response, even in the face of persecution.

Thus, it is through teaching, modeling, and counseling that people grow in Christ. By actually attempting to live the Kingdom life, and dealing with failures, natural discipleship occurs. All of this should not happen in isolation, but rather in concert with church development (because the people *are* the church).

Discipleship is a messy second phase, and it's one that is never really finished. As new believers come into the fellowship through evangelism, discipleship is needed. This ongoing cycle will eventually include the main phase: church development. That phase requires much more cooperation from the mission team, as that is where new teachers and evangelists are identified and trained, in hopes of raising up even a next generation apostle.

Kenya, in Pictures

The Carrier Family, February 2016

The weekly Wazee meeting

*A former Muslim imam, baptizing his neighbor into Christ
with Timothy*

Marc and Glenn Roseberry, with church wazee,
ordaining a deacon and an evangelist

Malnourished children in our feeding program,
with their caregivers and our deacon at the nutritionist

Foot washing at Communion: Titus on the right

Chapter 7: Church Development

Because of Titus, the message of the Kingdom reached a wider audience. Because of the discipleship process, we were able to keep the tares out of the wheat to a much greater degree, such that we finally introduced the main phase of a sustainable reproducible mission: *house church*! We were unsuccessful the first time because it was just *church in a house*. The second time, it was actually a gathering of people who were *called out* from the world. Though it wasn't perfect, we had something for sure.

There is actually some overlap between the second and third phases of a pioneer mission (discipleship and church development) because the process of discipleship is ongoing, and church development happens as believers are encouraged to exercise their gifts in the context of fellowship. Unfortunately, the first phase (evangelism) is the most exciting, so it's easy to want to short-change or neglect the next steps.

Evangelism and taking people into the Kingdom (repentance and baptism) creates a certain thrill, as you see God's Kingdom expand. An indigenous team or short-term missionaries involved in such work are thus easy to keep motivated. (There was a big difference between my initial short term teachings in Kenya and what I experienced on-the-ground a few years later!)

Training seminars, crusades (open air meetings), healing services, and conferences are blitz events that offer seeming breakthroughs and result in positive reports, but these occur in the "honeymoon phase" and the unfortunate reality is that without following up with the next steps of discipleship and church development (which are long-term commitments), many of these events have little to no lasting impact. Ongoing discipleship is the key to true spiritual growth, and house church is an essential element in the process.

On more than one occasion we have gone months with a total stop on all new evangelism or engagement of new sites. Whenever our groups seem like they're "a mile wide and an inch deep," or if people are going out in the evangelism phase but neglecting the spiritual disciplines, we regroup and focus on discipleship. If we lack teachers to handle the discipleship, I refocus on leadership development. When we staff up to meet the new workload, we then go back on the evangelism blitz and repeat the cycle. We go through all the phases in a predictable cycle on the mission field. A good leader makes iterative changes and keeps things flowing smoothly in the field and out to the disciples.

A smooth flow happens in the context of house church: sharing testimonies, experiencing confession, repentance, and restoration through communion, and members using their gifts for the benefit of the body. I've already talked about some aspects of house church at length, so I don't feel there's much more to say about that here. But the form of the church meetings themselves is not *the end—* there's one more important step. From among the membership of a strong church, leaders must be appointed so that the fellowship will stay strong and continue to grow. Eventually, either large fellowships will split into multiple fellowships, or new fellowships will be planted.

In order to have a sustainable and reproducible mission, this indigenous leadership *must* be developed such that they can repeat with the next generation everything that has been invested in them. Though Satan may lose some souls to the Kingdom, he is not threatened by your work if you are unable to generate leaders who can reproduce the mission, from evangelism to disciple-making and church-planting. A one-generation mission is no threat to him; frankly, neither is Great Commandment work that does not result in the spread of the gospel. However, when this transition of leadership is imminent, I believe Satan knows that this is the most important juncture of a mission and will do everything he can to interrupt this vital step.

Twice (once during our third year, and once during the fourth year), when we had begun to implement strategic leadership development initiatives, emerging leaders attempted coups that resulted in the church being shaken and the leadership development process stalled.

During the first such incident, an *mzee* recognized as a leader (due to having been a former pastor, though never ordained by us) was collaborating with others to, in his own words, force me out and take over the mission. He had planned to find a "good *mzungu* like Glenn Roseberry" (who they incorrectly assumed distributed benefits indiscriminately to church members). During this power play, one of the *mzee*'s supposed co-conspirators ratted him out; he even recorded one of the illicit meetings, which was shared with mission leadership.

After hearing and discussing the audio, the leadership confronted the *mzee* at his home. We asked him whether or not he had been plotting with others to push me out of the village (and the mission), and conspiring to take over the church. He, of course, denied the charges and kept demanding that we tell him who told us such "nonsense." We tried repeatedly to get an honest confession but he kept denying any culpability. Then I pulled out my computer and portable speakers and played the recorded conversation.

The *mzee* nervously squirmed in his chair for twenty minutes as everyone listened to his very distinct voice say all the things he insisted he had never said. Busted! As the recording finished he quickly shouted, "I confess, I did it and I repent!"

I calmly told him that just forty minutes earlier he had denied the meeting even occurred, never mind the truth of the coup conspiracy. Therefore, he had no remorse for what he had done, but rather only remorse that he had been caught. His wife burst out in tears, lamenting, "He has done this six times before—in every church we have attended!" How that fact escaped our vetting, only the

Lord knows! I gave him a stern warning to steer clear of the mission, and he has kept to himself ever since.

In both instances of quasi-leaders rising up due to personal ambitions, the core disciples persevered and ultimately the mission was restored. Of course, this occurred with no small amount of blood, sweat and tears on the part of mission leadership. If you're on the mission field, be prepared for the inevitable. As soon as you are at a pivotal juncture in the mission (such as in appointing indigenous leaders), Satan will attack: sometimes from outside, and (in our experience), sometimes from inside.

As in the New Testament examples of the Pauline churches, the ultimate goal of apostolic leadership is to appoint pastoral leaders to oversee and shepherd the disciples. However, these men do not just fall off trees—they need to be developed. An apostolic mission can transition to indigenous leaders once qualified and proven teachers, overseers, and deacons emerge.

Teachers are itinerant workers who are quickly identified by their zeal for the message and with the ease by which they are able to learn and teach. These disciples, however, need to be vetted for motive or agenda. We had one talented teacher with us for multiple years who was even ordained, only to discover that all the little warning signs we had seen through the years were indeed God-given red flags that we should have heeded.

Questions a pioneer missionary should ask about these young apprentices before they are given too much responsibility: are they reading their Bibles and praying on their own? Are they engaged in the work with personal initiative, or only "taking orders"? If married, is their spouse on board? A tell-tale sign of an unengaged disciple is a man whose wife does not also (eventually) surrender to the Kingdom. Sure, there are exceptions, but if a man is living the Kingdom life, it is usually attractive to his wife and she can be persuaded to the truth. Exercising discernment in assessing disciples with leadership potential is not *judging*, though it can appear so. Instead, it is a practical necessity in order to determine where to invest your time and resources.

An important, but sometimes overlooked, teacher who must be recognized in the fellowship is one or more older women who will teach the younger women, in accordance with Titus 2. This task has proven the most difficult in our village mission. The main issues have been lack of availability of first-generation women who know English, and lack of a good woman translator. After some starts and stops, we finally have an indigenous Kenyan leading the weekly women's meeting. However, the busy-ness of life for village women keeps regular attendance low. To supplement, we host an annual women's conference in our village. Women are invited from every church for an all-day conference, in which my wife Cindy teaches exclusively on women's issues. It has been life-transforming for many women and hopefully encourages them to continue to meet together on a more regular basis at their locations.

Early on in the Kenya mission, I created simple tracts that are used to train prospects consistently and ensure that a certain foundation is being laid during the discipleship process.[6] We teach these tracts based on a slightly modified acronym used by missiologists: *Model, Assist, Watch,* and *Let go* (MAWL). In this process, candidates learn to present the teaching booklets to others. As they do so, they are being discipled in their personal knowledge and spiritual growth, *and* they are being equipped to replicate the evangelism and discipleship processes to expand the church. It is essential that any aspiring church leader be able to share the Kingdom gospel and lead others in surrender, repentance, and baptism.

According to this acronym, first, you *Model*: teach the gospel of the Kingdom (using book one) and they watch. In the *Assist* phase, you and the student co-teach, the instructor stepping in when the disciple goes blank or makes substantive errors. In the *Watch* phase, the disciple teaches and the mentor keeps quiet. After enough practice, the aspiring evangelist is "signed off" by his mentor and can teach independently (*Let go*).

When it comes to leadership development, remember: *you can't learn to ride a bicycle in a seminar*. Practical application is necessary for most things, especially field evangelism and teaching. Thus, for the purposes of both discipleship and training, we go through all four of our field tracts with our disciples. This takes prospects through the Kingdom gospel (where some stop), and then through confession, repentance and baptism, and on to the specific teachings of Jesus. We end with *What Does the Bible Say About Church?* as the basis for organizing home fellowships.

Once trained and evaluated on actual teaching ability and delivery, we sit with the disciples and prepare for field readiness. In a group setting, we go over the most common objections (20 or so) and see how they are handled. Every field evangelist must be able to handle each and every objection proficiently using the Scriptures. Then we take them into the field and repeat MAWL with real prospects. Once verified, we have another field team!

During my second, and even third, years, using the MAWL method proved to be a challenge. I was the only instructor and did not know Swahili. That meant that either only English-speakers could be certified as teachers, or we had to use a translator during every phase of this long-term discipleship. Both options were very unnatural and limiting. However, once a core group of disciples was developed and strong teachers emerged, taking it to the next generation was much easier and more natural. Now, our Swahili-speaking disciples are trained

---

[6] This set of four booklets is freely available, along with other resources, at www.Kingdomdriven.org/Kingdom-resources.

by Swahili-speaking instructors, and I am just around to answer questions and confirm readiness for the field.

Elder development has surprisingly proven more difficult, primarily because most of our older men were polygamous prior to baptism. Yet that does not stop us from training them all. Here in Kenya, all old men are called *wazee* and, even if they don't meet the biblical qualifications of an overseer, they are esteemed because of their life experience and wisdom. All of our *wazee* participate in various leadership decisions and are a formidable gathering when addressing inevitable church discipline issues. However, only those who meet the biblical qualifications are appointed as overseers.

Our *wazee* training is centered on a weekly *wazee* meeting which rotates from house church to house church. Our regular attendance is approximately twenty men from four to six house churches. I attend these meetings, but they typically lead the discussions. Currently we are working our way through the Discovery Bible Study[7] series, with a different person facilitating each week.

The DBS is employed and referenced by multiple missiologists, as its use is common practice. However, the main inspiration for our use in the field is the writings of David and Paul Watson in *Contagious Disciple Making*. With their teachings as a framework, we in turn developed our own Bible study guide with a distinctive Kingdom perspective. (Notes on teaching the DBS are part of Appendix A: *Pioneer Mission Resources Checklist*).

My takeaway of the DBS premise is that information retention is rather poor through verbal teaching alone. Adding audiovisual aids can increase retention a bit. Reading, even more. Yet, interaction with the information (that is, actual discussion), will greatly increase the participants' understanding and application. In fact, following interaction, each individual's retention becomes the sum total of the group's collective memories. That has profound implications on carrying a teaching forward to successive generations. The DBS has been an integral part of the discipleship process and we use it in all our weekly meetings (youth, *wazee*, and women).

However, the *wazee* meetings, in particular, are much more than just meeting for Bible study (though that is important). They actually serve several purposes: One, they are a great encouragement to the brethren; two, they are a huge boost in credibility for the host church (the endorsement of so many *wazee* speaks to the community!); third, the meetings are an opportunity to constantly recast the vision and firm up our foundation. Lastly, this is where the *wazee* are assessed for their teaching ability and considered for being sent to an outside mission. (They will either be sent out as part of a two-by-two team for evangelism, or will

---

[7] The *Discovery Bible Study* is freely available at www.Kingdomdriven.org/Kingdom-resources.

be one of two teachers sent to strengthen the foundations in a fledgling fellowship.)

One challenge of leading a pioneer mission as an outsider, is that often bad feelings get stirred up, no matter how much you try to avoid it. A biblical church following Jesus' teachings on church discipline will invariably result in people being put out of the fellowship, who will then be very vocal against the mission and its leadership. This is just one more reason why it is so vital to develop a committee of strong indigenous leaders to share in decision-making. When decisions are made by a group of local leaders, it is much harder for ill-will to be directed toward them than it is toward a *mzungu* outsider. These leaders may be formally recognized overseers, or they may be "overseers-in-training."

These trusted advisors are not arbitrarily chosen. We've learned to take as much time as needed to thoroughly vet and test each candidate. They are evaluated for wisdom and decision-making ability, lack of bias, and reliance on Scripture rather than personal insight. They must be humble and not on a quest for power. And it goes without saying that they are of proven character.

From among the *wazee*, I have carefully monitored the men for an extended period of time for the above-referenced qualities. A few have been selected for deeper, private teachings. They are being specifically trained for conflict resolution, problem-solving, church discipline, shepherding and counseling, and dealing with many of the common challenges faced in the mission. Such challenges include but are not limited to: absent members, sin issues, conflicts and disputes, funerals and weddings, and so on. We teach the Scriptures, do drill and practice, and present all sorts of challenging scenarios to see how they would respond. After training, those meeting the qualifications for overseers (set forth in Titus 1 and 1 Timothy 3) are presented to the church as candidates for ordination. If the church ratifies their qualifications, they are formally ordained. This process, by necessity, takes time—but it is worth the investment.

The importance of this process is multi-faceted. As early as possible, the indigenous members must look to their peers as leaders. Ultimately, it is the local church that picks its own leaders. Though Scripture is clear that itinerant workers should appoint overseers, be mindful that this was not done in a vacuum. An itinerant worker only has superficial knowledge of a person's character, as compared to community peers in a local church. The qualifications set forth in Scripture are not all clearly observed by someone not living closely with the candidate. Therefore, the itinerant worker must observe and assess, yes, but simply for screening. Prospective candidates will likely need some focused training, but once they are presented as candidates, it will be the local church that makes the final assessment for ordination.

After teachers and overseers, deacons are the third group of leaders that must be ordained in order to have the next generation proliferate. KDM policy does not permit itinerant workers or even overseers to handle money (beyond for mission expenses); deacons alone are vetted for that task. As Scripture indicates, deacons are first tested to see if they are trustworthy—this is nowhere more significant than in dealings with money. We take this process slowly, giving potential deacons small opportunities to prove faithful, see the response, and raise the bar. We watch their personal lives, assess their spending habits, and ensure that their personal finances are in order. Honesty and integrity are vital characteristics for anyone in church leadership, especially deacons. If they have proven faithful, the leadership can present them to the church for official appointment.

The structure of our house churches gives potential deacons a training ground for such assessment. We permit even fledgling churches to take offerings, yet with guidelines: three disciples are selected from among the church to administer the collections. Offerings are taken in a concealed container and counted by the three selected disciples after the fellowship. The total is logged in a book, which remains publicly accessible to the baptized members. The money may be utilized in accordance with church policy (for food, clothing, medicine, burials...), as agreed upon by the three deacons-in-training. Our policy also allows indigenous leadership to be compensated if agreed upon by the church, with the candidate in question abstaining from participation in the vote. The apostolic leadership can periodically assess how the church is doing. All money collected in a local church returns to the members of the local church.

Deacons are a vital part of a Kingdom mission; they administer food assistance, organize medical treatment, and take care of details surrounding burials. Our deacons also collect special offerings for urgent needs. KDM policy is for the local fellowship to first try to solve their own problem. If the need is too great, they contact the deacon, who organizes a multi-church collection. If the emergency need is still unmet, KDM may solicit stateside donors by providing the details in a report and allowing people to give, if they desire.

In our mission, the number of disciples who fall away because of temptations in the area of money is high (it's not for no reason that 1 Timothy 6:10 says, "the love of money is a root of all sorts of evil, and some by longing for it have wandered away from the faith and pierced themselves with many griefs"). The easiest way to steal is by tampering with or "losing" receipts or cash. Taking cash and not doing the work is another method of theft. Our solution to this problem is to send people two-by-two. It certainly adds to the cost of taking patients to the hospital, for example, but safeguards the integrity of our spending and removes what might amount to an irresistible temptation. Deacons are the only people approved for handling cash without a second pair of eyes; however, they are required to keep logs of expenses and receipts, when applicable.

Every mission will face challenges in appointing indigenous leadership, and depending on the culture, these problems will vary. No matter the specific problems, a wise suggestion for the leadership development phase: *do not be hasty with the laying on of hands*, and have the church ratify the decision. First and second generation appointments may prove difficult because the church might lack the depth to stand firm on publicly assessing a candidate. (This is especially true in the case of a young church, which is why it doesn't hurt to take time during this phase.) In time, with authentic disciples doing the vetting, the risks of appointing leadership reduce somewhat.

No pioneer missionary will exit the mission, unless it's in the capable hands of next generation apostles and local overseers. If unqualified disciples assume leadership of the mission, the results for the disciples and churches will be disastrous. Thus, this leadership development phase of the pioneer mission is key to the reproducibility of the mission—it's part of the third and main phase in our four-phase, pioneer mission.

Chapter 8: Workers in the Harvest Field

Even if you're not in a situation where an attempted coup like I've described is likely, church leadership is still well spelled-out in the Scriptures and is a necessity, on or off the mission field. Proper church function depends on having the right people in the right places.

In our post-Christian culture, there is no small confusion about the apostolic mission, since the Western concept of "planting" a church usually just means opening up a building and selecting a pastor. However, there is a big difference between an apostle and a pastor, as well as confusion about other biblically-sanctioned roles and responsibilities within the church.

Christ commanded us to make disciples; He said He would build His church. He Himself is the cornerstone, and the foundation is of the apostles and prophets; the building (that is, the people) are being fitted together into the temple of God. Therefore, *Christ* is where the work of the apostles and prophets begins. Yet the foundation is on the apostles and prophets themselves: the appointed and sent ones, and those who hear the Lord's voice:

> So then you are no longer strangers and aliens, but you are fellow citizens with the saints, and are of God's household, having been built on the foundation of the apostles and prophets, Christ Jesus Himself being the corner *stone,* in whom the whole building, being fitted together, is growing into a holy temple in the Lord…(Ephesians 2:19-20)

The apostle Paul references this once again in 1 Corinthians 3:10-14:

> [10] According to the grace of God which was given to me, like a wise master builder I laid a foundation, and another is building on it. But each man must be careful how he builds on it. [11] For no man can lay a foundation other than the one which is laid, which is Jesus Christ. [12] Now if any man builds on the foundation with gold, silver, precious stones, wood, hay, straw, [13] each man's work will become evident; for the day will show it because it is *to be* revealed with fire, and the fire itself will test the quality of each man's work. [14] If any man's work which he has built on it remains, he will receive a reward.

Paul, as a master builder (being an appointed and sent one) laid a foundation, of which Christ was the cornerstone. He says others were building on the foundation he had laid. Who are these other people? Why and when did he relinquish construction to others?

Let's look at the general way in which Paul operated; for example, a mission with Barnabas. The two men publicly preached and then withdrew to the privacy of the man of peace's home. There, those who surrendered and repented were baptized and a church was birthed. Paul picked up several disciples along the way, as well as mentioning others in his letters to the churches. These named individuals were sometimes given direction for how they could help Paul; at other times, they accompanied him for their own training purposes. Paul might remain in one location for a season; however, due to persecution he was often forced to move on quickly. Yet he still sent teachers and letters to strengthen the churches he had planted. All this can be discerned by surveying the Book of Acts in unison with the Pauline epistles.

Based on this information, one might assume that Paul's co-laborers (the next generation of appointed and sent ones, such as Timothy) may have been the ones who took over building on the apostolic foundation. However, Paul actually specifies who these new builders were:

> [11] And He gave some *as* apostles, and some *as* prophets, and some *as* evangelists, and some *as* pastors and teachers, [12] for the equipping of the saints for the work of service, to the building up of the body of Christ; [13] until we all attain to the unity of the faith, and of the knowledge of the Son of God, to a mature man, to the measure of the stature which belongs to the fullness of Christ. (Ephesians 4:10-13)

Here we see what is commonly known as "the five-fold ministry" (see also 1 Corinthians 12:28). These are the workers most responsible for building on the foundation, which is Christ. We will get to the additional "builders" referenced in this passage, but first let's elaborate a bit more on the foundation-builders: apostles and prophets. Some understand these two together in reference to the witness of the Old and New Testaments. However, this proves very odd since Paul himself was writing the passages, long before the New Testament was compiled.

In the context of the primitive church, the original Greek meanings were easily understood; *apostles* were those individuals who were called and sent. Some today will argue that this includes only the Twelve. Where, then, does Paul fit in? And if Paul is the one special exception, what about his co-laborers? Where do we draw the line between those who *were* apostles, and those who aren't? If the five-fold giftings were given "until we all attain to the unity of the faith, and of the knowledge of the Son of God, to a mature man, to the measure of the stature which belongs to the fullness of Christ," do you think we have achieved that goal yet?

Likewise, if the foundational prophets simply refer to the Old Testament, who are the prophets that we are told should be speaking in the average house church service? (See 1 Corinthians 14.) The meaning is clear: the original Greek usage of *sent ones* and *prophets* were (and are) no doubt instrumental roles in laying the foundation of the church in an ongoing sense, not just limited to a specific group of people, or an arbitrarily delineated time in history.

So what is the role of prophet in the New Testament church? Prophesy is simply hearing from the Lord. The Lord speaks to His church to provide guidance, warnings, and sometimes correction. He speaks through dreams, visions, signs, and sometimes a timely word. For some He is obvious and overt.

For others he is very subtle and quiet. It is through the agency of the prophets that He directly intervenes in the body life of His *ekklesia*.

I can give you countless examples of visions and dreams given to disciples, oftentimes with the meaning obscured, just for another brother to interpret the dream such that it is unveiled and then obvious for all to see. The Lord has given multiple timely warnings to our churches when conspiracies were being concocted. Through His direct involvement, serious situations were thwarted.

When I received a credible death threat, *seven* different disciples came to me with dreams or visions of the imminent danger, though I had told no one about it. We prayed and fasted and then the Lord gave me a specific vision that was interpreted to mean that the threat was released. I pity all the saints and churches who fail to take advantage of the gifts of the Spirit and revelation through the gift of prophecy. Our mission would have failed a long time ago without His very direct guidance. As the Scriptures say, the church is built on the foundation of the apostles and prophets, not the wisdom or hard work of men.

Thus, the apostles and prophets are clearly the foundation-builders of the church. Moving on in those key verses, we see in the five-fold ministry three others mentioned: evangelists, pastors and teachers. Evangelists have already been discussed a bit throughout this book (the 70 "appointed and sent" ones); let us shelve them temporarily and come back to them later in brief. For now, let's talk about pastors and teachers. Teachers may be itinerant or settled in one location, depending on the phase of the mission: apostolic or pastoral. Disciples who are gifted at teaching, teach whether the church is new or mature, and may move from place to place (as those Paul sent to the various churches).

Pastors are clearly a local role. The New Testament and very early church role of such leaders is remarkably dissimilar from what we see in modern traditional churches. First of all, we must differentiate (or rather combine) the roles of pastor, elder, and overseer (bishop). So let us go to the Greek.

Poimen, translated pastor or shepherd, is just that, a herdsman. *Presbuteros*, translated elder or presbyter, is an older person. *Episkopos*, translated overseer or bishop, is a man charged with seeing that things to be done by others are done rightly. Note that pastor refers to an office in the Ephesians 4:11 list. Yet this term (in noun form) is used only this one time in reference to a church leader. Yet elsewhere the word is used in verb form (*poimaino*).

> Therefore, I exhort the <u>elders</u> among you, as *your* fellow <u>elder</u> and witness of the sufferings of Christ, and a partaker also of the glory that is to be revealed, [2] <u>shepherd</u> the flock of God among you, <u>exercising oversight</u> not under compulsion, but voluntarily, according to *the will of* God; and not for sordid gain, but with eagerness; [3] nor yet as lording it over those allotted to your charge, but proving to be examples to the flock. (1 Peter 5:1-3)

The word (for shepherd or pastor) was used to describe the responsibilities of a *presbuteros* (older man), who were also tasked to oversee (the verb form of *episkopos*) the church. We note that Peter is an apostle, but refers to himself as a *presbuteros*, clearly indicating that he is meaning the common usage of the Greek word, older man. This is absolutely clear if you continue reading the passage until verse 5, where Peter makes an obvious contrast between the role of younger men and older men. My point here is that shepherding (pastoring) is simply a responsibility of the older men, as is overseeing the affairs of the church.

A second example is found in Acts 20:17-28. In verse 17, Paul called the *presbuteros* (older men) of the church to see him. We then read Paul's instructions to the older men in verse 28:

> [28] Be on guard for yourselves and for all the flock, among which the Holy Spirit has made you <u>overseers,</u> to <u>shepherd</u> the church of God which He purchased with His own blood.

Again, the older men were said to be made *episkopos* (overseers) and to shepherd (*poimaino*) the church. Therefore, it is a subset of older men, those who are made overseers of the church by the Holy Spirit, who are tasked with shepherding the church. Previously we saw that itinerant workers are set apart and called by the Holy Spirit; yet they were appointed through the laying on of hands of a local church. Now, in the verse above, we see local church leaders are also made overseers by the Holy Spirit. So who appoints them?

On Paul and Barnabas's first apostolic (Luke 10 evangelism) mission (recorded in Acts 13:1 to 14:28), they were set apart by the Holy Spirit, appointed and sent by the church, and publicly preached the Kingdom to the crowds. Yet upon rejection and persecution, they moved on from place to place, even literally wiping the dust off their feet as Christ commanded in Luke 10 (Acts 13:51). Though rejected by the masses, the men of peace emerged, many disciples were made, and fledgling churches were birthed. The exact time involved in this mission is unknown, yet it is speculated to have taken multiple years. They later returned to the churches and strengthened them (Acts 14:22-23). Then: "When they had appointed elders for them in every church, having prayed with fasting, they commended them to the Lord in whom they had believed" (Acts 14:23). It was the apostles Barnabas and Paul (see Acts 14:14) who appointed qualified older men as overseers to shepherd the churches. Then the apostles spent a long time with the disciples (Acts 14:28). This is a model Luke 10 mission.

What are these qualifications? All appointed overseers are older men, but not all older men are appointed as overseers to shepherd the churches. Therefore, from among the older men, Paul specified that certain criteria must be met, as validated by the church. We see a perfect example of this in Paul's instructions to his apprentice apostle Titus:

[5] For this reason I left you in Crete, that you would set in order what remains and appoint <u>elders</u> in every city as I directed you, [6] *namely*, if any man is above reproach, the husband of one wife, having children who believe, not accused of dissipation or rebellion. [7] For the <u>overseer</u> must be above reproach as God's steward, not self-willed, not quick-tempered, not addicted to wine, not pugnacious, not fond of sordid gain, [8] but hospitable, loving what is good, sensible, just, devout, self-controlled, [9] holding fast the faithful word which is in accordance with the teaching, so that he will be able both to exhort in sound doctrine and to refute those who contradict. (Titus 1:5-9)

Paul did his Luke 10 work in Crete. Then he had his apprentice apostle remain behind to set affairs in order; specifically; appointing older men who met the qualifications he specified to be overseers of the church. That was his "remaining work." It was Paul's handoff to those who would build on the apostolic and prophetic foundation. Their work would be the work later tested by fire, to see if it would endure. It is the shift from apostolic to pastoral ministry.

So what is the apostle's role after handing over leadership to indigenous disciples? As recommended by Peter in the admonition for older men in 1 Peter 5:1-3, Paul tried to lead by setting an example. He even said as much:

[5] For we never came with flattering speech, as you know, nor with a pretext for greed—God is witness— [6] nor did we seek glory from men, either from you or from others, even though as apostles of Christ we might have asserted our authority. [7] But we proved to be gentle among you, as a nursing *mother* tenderly cares for her own children. (1 Thessalonians 2:5-7)

Although there were very few instances where Paul exerted his apostolic authority, it did happen. He rebuked churches for wavering beliefs (Galatians 3:1-4), for disunity (1 Corinthians 1:10-17), and for not following Jesus' teachings on church discipline (1 Corinthians 5); in the latter case, he pronounced judgment himself because the church failed to. But his primary role was to send teachers, send letters with teachings and encouragement, pray unceasingly, and visit them when he was able.

So what are the qualifications of an itinerant worker, whether an apostle, evangelist, or teacher? We see in the Scriptures that appointed and sent ones were ordained by some criteria not specified. In order to determine what their qualifications were, and therefore how to develop or recognize such individuals, we will have to peruse the New Testament.

Paul referred to himself as a preacher, an apostle and a teacher (1 Timothy 2:7, 2 Timothy 1:11). We can infer that a sent one may also have the gifts of teaching and preaching, though it may just be true in Paul's case. Note that a preacher is a *herald* or a *public proclaimer* of the gospel to the unsaved. That is *not* akin to the modern understanding of *preacher*, which is someone who gives a sermon at a Sunday morning service in a religious building. Read the Book of Acts and you will understand what Paul meant by being a preacher; preaching is for unbelievers, and teaching is for the church. Paul was gifted in both of these areas.

Paul was likewise not one of the Twelve, though he had seen the Lord. His apostolic ministry was apparently contested by some. Yet his apostleship was validated by the fruit of his mission: "If to others I am not an apostle, at least I am to you; for you are the seal of my apostleship in the Lord" (1 Corinthians 9:12).

Paul was clearly *not* pastoring churches. He pioneered new ground, preached the Kingdom, made new disciples, developed leaders, and then strengthened and shepherded the churches himself, and with the team of other apostles he had trained. He led that team even from his house arrest. *That* is fruit of apostleship!

Some more detail is given in Scripture concerning the foreign travelers, what we would today call *missionaries* in the original sense of the word. We note that Paul and Barnabas were unmarried men at the time of their mission work. Early church writings detail that most of Paul's co-laborers were also single. Therefore, these men were not required to comply with the qualifications specified for church overseers and deacons ("husband of one wife"). We see in Scripture that Timothy, though ordained, was a *young man*, yet of requisite character (1 Timothy 4:12-14), in contrast to the qualification of an overseer, who must be an older man. Therefore, an itinerant worker (apostle, teacher, or evangelist) could be young or old, single or married.

We see some of the duties of an itinerant worker (an evangelist or teacher) in Paul's instructions to Timothy and Titus. These men were next-generation workers personally trained by Paul, and referred to as his children in the faith. Being young and single, Timothy certainly did not meet the qualifications of a church overseer, even though these latter letters of Paul are often referred to as the "pastoral letters." Paul specifically referred to Timothy as an evangelist (2 Timothy 4:5). He was commanded to prescribe and teach sound doctrine, publicly reading the Scriptures (1 Timothy 4). Yet, it was not in one location (hence, itinerant).

It was these itinerant workers who were tasked with leadership development (2 Timothy 2:2) and appointment (Titus 1:5). It was Timothy and Titus who were commanded to appoint overseers and deacons in the churches from among the disciples. Paul simply provided them with lists of qualifications and left them to do the task (1 Timothy 3:1-13 and Titus 1:5-9). They were given the task of setting the churches in order through teaching and shepherding. They were given authority to rebuke elders who would not repent, but only if their sin was validated by multiple witnesses (1 Timothy 5:19-21). To avoid such occurrences, they were told "not be hasty with the laying on of hands" (1 Timothy 5:22). They were also given authority to reject divisive men after two warnings (Titus 3:10-11). They were instructed to tell the saints how to conduct themselves based on gender, age and other roles or status. They traveled from church to church doing just that:

> I solemnly charge *you* in the presence of God and of Christ Jesus, who is to judge the living and the dead, and by His appearing and His Kingdom: preach the word; be ready in season *and* out of season; reprove, rebuke, exhort, with great patience and instruction. (2 Timothy 4:2)

The "learners" that we have previously discussed in detail (the sent ones in Luke 9 and 10) were sent as evangelists and healers, and no details were given in the Scriptures of any other activities. Quite simply, they would remain with the man of peace for some days and simply proclaim the Kingdom message. No specific qualifications for these evangelists are mentioned. However, they likely would be expected to be of proven character, as were the young man Timothy and Titus. They would also need to teach sound doctrine, as Paul instructed Timothy. (We have already noted that Paul recognized this young man as an evangelist.)

Through the New Testament writings, we see how the church should function: the foundation of Christ is laid by the apostles and prophets. The foundation is built upon by teachers (itinerant or local), pastors, and evangelists—those named as part of the "five-fold ministry." These workers function to build up the saints and equip them for works of service. Once this is accomplished, the cycle can be repeated again and the church will continue to grow.

The topic of church leadership (particularly the five-fold ministry, as it is called) is a deep one, yet vital to understand if a pioneer mission is to succeed. In the last chapter, the necessity of launching indigenous leaders in the developing fellowships has naturally led to this discussion of what the qualifications and definitions are for such men. Perhaps this has been somewhat of an interlude, but it completes the picture for the third, and arguably most important, aspect of the pioneer mission: church development.

Chapter 9: Changes and Challenges

Shortly following a season of rapid growth late in our second year (originating with the *wazee*), a second *mzungu* family joined us in the village. This family had a burden for Great Commandment[8] work, as compared to the Great Commission work I had pioneered. This variance in gifting and focus was envisioned as being complementary as we prepared for their integration in the mission. In fact, I considered such works to be an essential fourth phase in the pioneer mission.

Unfortunately, we did not have a well-thought-out plan as to how the desired programs would be integrated, nor was communication between all parties optimal for a smooth transition. The rumor mill and resulting expectations in the village also rather "forced" the new Great Commandment works to be implemented in an unforeseen manner that was not ideal. By no fault of any of the well-intentioned workers, the dynamic created by the change in focus would also prove to be a serious disruption to the ongoing apostolic mission.

We had always cared for any of the sick who came to us, as well as fed the hungry as they were brought to our attention. However, this was a one-by-one process which usually involved our "gatekeeper," Titus. Patients were screened, their stories checked, and their condition pre-qualified to meet the treatment criteria. Titus would usually be the one to take them to the clinic, and we would simply pay the bill at the end of the month. That system was immediately a thing of the past when the new *wazungu* arrived.

We quickly found out that everyone thought a medical clinic was starting right there in our compound! Leading up to the arrival of the second *wazungu* family, we might have treated a few patients each week, with some down-time between each. However, the day they came, there were literally a dozen people with medical problems suddenly lined up at our gate, waiting. The number per day went up from there, and we had to figure out on-the-fly how to deal with the crisis. Not enough staff, not enough money, not enough hours in the day. No time for "settling in" for this family—it was sink or swim! This put a lot of pressure on everyone.

After two years in the village, and willingly dealing with all kinds of foot traffic and many different needs, our family was now forced to deal with a new dynamic. Total strangers were walking into our compound at will to speak to the *mzungu* "doctor" and get free medical treatment. For them, it was a gift from God. Yet for our families' privacy and security, it was an absolute disaster.

---

[8] By this, I mean service- or humanitarian-oriented works, engaged in as an outreach and in response to Jesus' command to "love your neighbor as yourself" (Matthew 22:39; see also Matthew 25:31-46).

One day, Titus (who often used his motorbike to transport patients to the local clinic) was hanging out in the yard, carefully observing all the people milling about waiting for their medical consultation. He noticed one young man wander away from the main group and begin to inspect our shed and private side yard. Titus, always our advocate, pretended to wash his motorbike while keeping an eye on this man, whom he had now recognized as one of a group of violent robbers in the village. The man did some reconnaissance and then walked out the gate, never waiting to see anyone about any medical problems.

Of course, Titus immediately brought the issue to my attention. It was not as if we had not already acknowledged problems with the current situation, but here we were put in a pinch. I had eight children at the time, all of whom wanted to play freely and securely in their own yard. The new *wazungu* family also had two young children. The constant influx of unknown visitors had to be stopped; we needed some organization!

We immediately set "clinic" days and hours and put out a certain number of chairs for visitors to the outdoor clinic area. Any overflow beyond the seating area was asked to stay outside the gate until there was space available inside. Eventually, we hired one of the brothers to act as security outside the gate and keep things flowing smoothly with everyone who wanted to be seen.

Disruption and inconvenience aside (practical matters which eventually were arranged to everyone's satisfaction), the ongoing clinic work ultimately had a unforeseen impact on the Kingdom gospel mission. Immediately, the villagers directly associated our home fellowship with the medical work being done in the same compound. Our Sunday home fellowship exploded to standing-room only. The bulk of "testimonies" would often simply be poorly-veiled accounts of the medical condition for which the visitors sought treatment. Numerous patients would walk to the clinic area immediately after fellowship.

As we strategized about how to address the visitors (hoping for some Kingdom impact), we began to offer teaching after fellowship to allow visitors to hear the Kingdom gospel; this was typically done by one of the indigenous disciples. Many of these visitors would apparently accept the message, only to find out later that they assumed their medical treatment was conditional upon church membership.

We quickly recognized the conflicts of interest and tried our best to mitigate the situation, but we were never able to recover, absent literally re-locating both the clinic and the fellowship location to an area off of the *mzungu* compound. Not only did we have ongoing problems with newcomers, but the pre-existing disciples also were very confused by what seemed to be a completely different mission from what they had experienced prior to the arrival of the medical clinic. Before, they were given the Word of God with no strings attached. Now they saw that the new *wazungu* came wielding benefits, like the majority of missionaries who had come before them.

As I've shared previously, East Africa has a long history of foreigners coming with the gospel, yes, but also hospitals, schools and many other material benefits. All of our *wazee* have personally experienced this phenomenon. Village rumors began freely flowing concerning all the wonderful things this Kingdom Driven Ministries (KDM) denomination would bring. Our zealous new converts would tell their family and friends in an effort to start new fellowships: token mention made of the Kingdom but much fanfare about all the benefits that accompanied KDM "membership."

As I tried to curb the undesired impact of the new dynamic, it created no little confusion among the disciples and conflict with the new family. These sincere believers were just trying to do the good things that God commanded us all to do. However, the new dichotomy of the mission change was, at best, confusing.

To my personal discouragement, several of the most trained and talented disciples that I had personally invested in were convinced that serving the needy was a more noble task than preaching the gospel. Some of my strongest evangelists and teachers were no longer available for missions, as they were volunteering to assist with medical needs. My push-back (in defense of the gospel work, which was being compromised) appeared to be an effort to prevent people from receiving vital assistance. These inaccurate assumptions were ill-received by both the disciples and the new family.

Eventually, the family moved on to another mission that was more consistent with their call, and the apostolic mission was set back on track through months of foundational re-teachings and continued discipleship. Those who had joined the church for reasons other than the Kingdom of God either simply slowly disappeared or were excommunicated as a result of unrepentant sins. (The *wazee* got lots of experience with Matthew 18!) In the end, the Lord severely purged the church. The entire experience ultimately proved very educational and beneficial to the mission, and once again, the disciples with good and honest hearts ultimately persevered through this challenging season.

In a nutshell, here's the lesson from this season: on a mission field where there are historic influences involving money or where there are temptations in that regard (which I would wager applies to a majority of developing nations), care must be exercised with Great Commandment work so as not to compromise the development of healthy churches. Think of the mission as a four-course meal, with the last dish being dessert. Your patrons might very much like (and prefer) dessert, but you want to serve the other three courses first. If they get dessert first, not only is it unhealthy for them, but it might fill them up, leaving no appetite for what should have come before it. In the same way, the Great Commandment work is a good "dessert" and a necessary component of the four-phase pioneer mission. Disciples need to see good works being done and learn to

85

participate in this aspect of Kingdom life. However, if served first, Great Commandment assistance threatens to sabotage the health of the mission as a whole.

The Great Commandment mission, which was always part of KDM's work, has now transitioned to the headship of trusted, indigenous disciples. We still provide medical assistance to the sick, food for the hungry and malnourished, and many other types of vital assistance. The difference is, those in need visit a facility that is not associated with *wazungu*; they consult with African staff; and they are assisted by Africans. Due to the size and nature of our village community, those seeking assistance are known to those who serve, so there is a realistic assessment of legitimate needs.

We now even have Africans interviewing patients, taking photographs, and writing reports to solicit donors when special cases arise. We *wazungu* are only consulted when unique cases emerge that are outside the specified treatment criteria. Of course, it's KDM partners who pay the bills. However, we look forward to a much more independent Kenya mission in the future. The Great Commandment, done *by* Africans *for* Africans…that is the apostolic vision of the Kingdom of God. We praise God for all of our experiences—even the difficult lessons—that have helped us focus on how to best implement the Great Commandment works that are an essential element of a Kingdom mission.

A valuable takeaway from all of this is that we remain focused on Jesus' priorities in our ministries, particularly in the work of the Great Commandment. We see that Jesus fed the multitudes in John 6. Very large crowds were following Him because of the healings they had heard reported. Seeing the crowd, He organized to miraculously feed them; they were all satisfied. The next day, crowds again gathered to Him. He addressed them with these words:

> [26]Jesus answered them and said, "Truly, truly, I say to you, you seek Me, not because you saw signs, but because you ate of the loaves and were filled. [27]Do not work for the food which perishes, but for the food which endures to eternal life, which the Son of Man will give to you, for on Him the Father, God, has set His seal." (John 6:26-27)

The people then argued with Jesus, trying to convince Him He should feed them as Moses did, because Moses gave free food. Jesus tried to explain to them that He Himself was what they really needed, and the food they sought would offer just a fleeting benefit. His focus was for them to receive eternal life, yet they were consumed with filling their bellies. In the end, they grumbled over His teachings, and most left him. The lesson, as applied to the Great Commandment, seems obvious: sometimes, such work is vital to the mission, but it shouldn't overshadow people's true spiritual needs. The human propensity will be to focus on what is temporal, but Jesus challenges us to seek that which is eternal.

Jesus left us another example that should not escape our notice: the healing of the ten lepers.

[11] While He was on the way to Jerusalem, He was passing between Samaria and Galilee. [12] As He entered a village, ten leprous men who stood at a distance met Him; [13] and they raised their voices, saying, "Jesus, Master, have mercy on us!" [14] When He saw them, He said to them, "Go and show yourselves to the priests." And as they were going, they were cleansed. [15] Now one of them, when he saw that he had been healed, turned back, glorifying God with a loud voice, [16] and he fell on his face at His feet, giving thanks to Him. And he was a Samaritan. [17] Then Jesus answered and said, "Were there not ten cleansed? But the nine— where are they? [18] Was no one found who returned to give glory to God, except this foreigner?" [19] And He said to him, "Stand up and go; your faith has made you well."

This is an important teaching. Jesus healed ten, yet only one returned to give glory to God. This example rings so true from our experiences helping people here in the village. Most people who received substantive benefits simply go on, and you will never see them again. We have seen negligible lasting Kingdom fruit from assisting people with physical needs. We certainly praise God for the one in ten, yet there is a serious bout of conscience with granting people momentary comfort, when we recognize that an eternity in Hell awaits them. Granted, sometimes doing good works is sowing seeds, which in the future other workers can reap. We do not know in full how God is working through different people and programs; even so, it is important to maintain a Kingdom focus in the work that is being done.

Certainly, those whose focus is Great Commandment work are (hopefully) doing what they do in obedience to Jesus. You can't go wrong there! Jesus commands us to love our neighbors as ourselves and to do to others what we want them to do to us. However, loving others does not always equate to indiscriminately helping them. Helping can hurt people! (I recommend all missionaries read *When Helping Hurts: How to Alleviate Poverty Without Hurting the Poor... and Yourself* to learn about this dynamic.) As with most issues, the Scriptures should guide us in determining what constitutes necessary assistance.

Jesus taught a story about the things His Father in heaven would provide for those who seek His Kingdom and His righteousness (see Matthew 6:25-34 and Luke 12:22-34). This I take as a promise from God: that if we seek His Kingdom and His righteousness, He will give us food and clothing (Luke adds drink). Likewise, James 2:14-17 instructs the believers,

[14] What use is it, my brethren, if someone says he has faith but he has no works? Can that faith save him? [15] If a brother or sister is without clothing and in need of daily food, [16] and one of you says to them, "Go in peace, be warmed and be filled," and yet you do not give them what is necessary for *their* body, what use is that? [17] Even so faith, if it has no works, is dead, *being* by itself. (James 2)

87

The hands and feet of Jesus in providing for the needs He promises are *the brethren*. If our brethren are in need of food and clothing, we are obligated to assist them. This does not speak about helping outsiders, and does not speak to non-necessities. It is a very restrictive passage. Furthermore, we read that the brethren are to be satisfied with these basic necessities and seek no more (see 1 Timothy 6:6-10)

The list of necessities is somehow lengthened in the criteria used to measure faithfulness at the judgment in Matthew 25:31-46:

> [35] For I was hungry, and you gave Me *something* to eat; I was thirsty, and you gave Me *something* to drink; I was a stranger, and you invited Me in; [36] naked, and you clothed Me; I was sick, and you visited Me; I was in prison, and you came to Me.' (Matthew 25)

We see that it is important, again, to provide food, drink, and clothing, but also lodging (in the form of hospitality) and visitation at critical times. Note that these are still all necessities. In context, remember that in Jesus' time (and in many nations today), prisoners and those in hospitals do not have their basic needs met; it is up to family or friends to provide these things regularly. Visiting prisoners and the sick, then, has a very practical application of supporting needy brethren during these seasons of challenge. The *least of these* in this passage is clearly stated as "these brothers of mine" in verse 40: "'Truly I say to you, to the extent that you did it to one of these brothers of Mine, *even* the least *of them*, you did it to Me.'" Again, the teaching remains consistent: we will be judged for not assisting brethren with the necessities of life.

Belonging to a Kingdom fellowship is not to become a chance for opportunists to get a free ride. In fact, Paul gave a stern warning that lazy people and busybodies were to be chastised by the church. He was quite blunt that if a man refuses to work, then neither shall he eat (2 Thessalonians 3:6-15).

What about people outside the church? Galatians 6:10 tells us, "So then, while we have opportunity, let us do good to all people, and especially to those who are of the household of the faith." It is vitally important to assist the desperately needy, both inside and outside the church. Jesus said, "Let your light shine before men in such a way that they may see your good works, and glorify your Father who is in heaven." (Matthew 5:16). One lesson learned on the mission field, however, is that these types of good works are best done person-to-person, rather than on an organizational basis, as much as is practicable.

Jesus modeled this in His story of the Good Samaritan (Luke 10:30-37). In this story, a man happens by a perfect stranger who is badly injured. He carries him to a facility for care and pays the bill. He doesn't open his own medical clinic, hire some staff, and provide medicine for every passerby. We have tried to follow this example with our medical missions as much as possible. Although medical treatment is not on the biblical necessity short list, we have seen that the ones Jesus sent out were told to "heal the sick." This was likewise the impetus for the story of the Good Samaritan. Certainly, praying for the sick is a vital starting point, and we *should* expect to see miraculous healings. However, assisting someone in getting medical treatment here is often seen as a miracle in itself, and it allows faraway brethren to put their compassion into practice by giving financially to these special needs.

The Great Commission includes the Great Commandment, which at some level must be modeled by those who are in the field doing the work of the mission. It is integral to the process of discipleship to provide opportunities for brethren to assist one another, as well as those outside the church: "[10] For we are His workmanship, created in Christ Jesus for good works, which God prepared beforehand so that we would walk in them." (Ephesians 2:10). Remember Ephesians 4:11-12?

> [11] And He gave some *as* apostles, and some *as* prophets, and some *as* evangelists, and some *as* pastors and teachers, [12] for the equipping of the saints for the work of service, to the building up of the body of Christ...

If the end-goal is to equip our indigenous disciples to meet the very pressing needs around them, it begs the question: how will they do that when the missionaries (and their funding) go away?

When Jesus fed the thousands, what did He say to His disciples?

> [15] When it was evening, the disciples came to Him and said, "This place is desolate and the hour is already late; so send the crowds away, that they may go into the villages and buy food for themselves." [16] But Jesus said to them, "They do not need to go away; you give them *something* to eat!" [17] They said to Him, "We have here only five loaves and two fish." [18] And He said, "Bring them here to Me."(Matthew 14:15-18)

Here the disciples saw a need; they immediately were overburdened by the enormity of that need. Yet Jesus told *them* to feed the crowds. They responded that they only had a little among them. Jesus told them to bring it, implying it was enough. This is what the Lord expects from all of us.

Assuming that God needs our [Westerners'] help in meeting needs is simply Western arrogance. God graciously offers us an opportunity to serve so that we can receive a blessing, storing treasures in Heaven, but if we do not participate, God will be glorified regardless. My personal belief as to why God does not miraculously heal everyone we pray for, is so that we can partake in meeting the need for our own personal blessing. Yet the opposite remains true: if we saints are not able to meet a need through the medical and pharmaceutical establishment, this is an invitation for God to directly meet that need. Let me give you an example.

A young boy (14 years) who was extremely sick and unresponsive was admitted to a quality, private hospital. He was the son of a very poor neighbor of Timothy's. (Remember Timothy, a brother salvaged from a corrupted fellowship? He was now the leader of a home fellowship!) At the time, our medical program was in crisis and I told Timothy there was nothing we could do to help financially. So we prayed for him. Within days he came to, and then fully recovered. Then, another miracle: the hospital waived the entire $3,600 bill! To this day, the boy testifies to these great miracles and serves God with all his heart. In fact, recently, the family was burdened with the fact he could not go to school because they could not afford school fees (school is not free here). So without disturbing anyone from the church or mission, they prayed. The boy received a full scholarship to an excellent school. If we Westerners had intervened and interfered in this work, *wazungu*, rather than God, would have been the recipient of the glory due Him.

Doing nothing is *not* nothing; it is an opportunity to allow God to work and reveal His power. And doing something is not nothing; it is an opportunity to serve the neediest and store treasures in Heaven. How wonderful it is to work in partnership with God! This is why it is so important to listen to the Lord's leading to understand His perfect will in every situation. We want to participate in the Lord's work, not pioneer our own.

These are some thoughts on the Great Commandment, and how the members of the body of Christ might work together to meet specific needs. Yet there is also a place for emergency intervention, where the social infrastructure is overwhelmed by some disaster. In these cases, the workers come, and they go. By being community-based, jealousy and any sense of personal entitlement are minimized (although communities can become jealous of other communities who received assistance if they did not). This type of scenario can be an excellent opportunity for service-oriented individuals to be the hands and feet of Jesus.

Apart from a true disaster that overwhelms the local infrastructure, however, it is usually best to allow the culture to address its own needs. It is our own disciples who constantly remind us that hand-outs result in laziness and complacency. Though people do struggle, they make it, and precious few are actually starving.

The disasters plaguing our region that most benefit from outside help, are the HIV and malaria pandemics. The other trend we see is the destruction of the family. When people marry, remarry, and father children out of wedlock, it leaves numerous people out of reach of the plentiful supplies of affordable food or safe housing.

Culturally here, if a widow or widower remarries (or if a man takes a second "wife"), their children are not received by the new spouse. Either they are treated as outcasts, with only very basic needs met, or they are sent to the care of grandparents or other family members. Street children, and many of the malnourished children we assist, are often among this disadvantaged group.

Truly these and other crises can only be solved with the gospel of the Kingdom and the life-changing teachings of Jesus. Many solutions just treat the symptoms, not the underlying problem.

Unfortunately, there will always be unmet needs such as these in developing nations. In fact, Jesus said, *we will always have the poor among us* (John 12:8). Focusing on the Great Commission prior to the Great Commandment seems counter-intuitive—but if that is our focus, people's priority need for spiritual wholeness will be the first served, thus inciting social change at a grassroots level. Where there continues to be needs, we will raise up a virtual army of workers who can do these works of service. *More* people will be helped, not less!

Each of us is gifted by God to perform a vital part of successful mission's work, whether the Great Commission or the Great Commandment. However, if one part is not working in concert with the others, the results will be unpredictable and, perhaps, undesirable. It is important to be cognizant of these two vital elements, and how they interact with one another, as you pursue the development of a sustainable, reproducible mission.

Chapter 10: Anticipating Potential Problems

The challenges of pioneer mission work come in so many forms from within and without, that it's only by God's grace that any of us can persevere unto fruitfulness in the field! With all the preparations we made prior to coming, it is still amazing how ill-prepared we were for the realities of the field. So where do I start?

Though we didn't know it when we embarked on our journey, we should probably have expected betrayal at some point. It usually happens in relation to money, but it might also be related to the missionary's foreign status and the fact that he's simply an "outsider." It happened to us before we even got off the plane. That betrayal, and others close on its heels, jaded our worldview (at least in the short term) and made trusting the people we were sent to minister to a challenge. It was certainly Satan's plan for us to struggle to trust, and as a result, to keep relationships at arm's length. Yet, we now know that these events (as with all struggles in life), were sent by God for a purpose. We learned the importance of believing the best in others, in the way of Christ's love. We learned to keep our hearts, and the relationships, open, while still being discerning of fruitfulness (particularly before committing financial resources). I don't know if missionaries in other developing nations need to be wary of this type of dynamic, but (unfortunately) this has certainly been my experience in East Africa.

Related to this was the challenge of developing authentic relationships (again, simply because of our foreign status). Based on some research, our observations, and impromptu interviews with our disciples, we've concluded that among the people group that we live with, relationships are generally a mile wide and an inch deep. Husbands, wives, and children have a rather functional existence, with few demonstrations of affection and, typically, a lack of deep conversation. This was somewhat explained when we read the book *African Friends and Money Matters* during our third year in Kenya. (I wish I had gotten my hands on a copy much sooner!)

I can't offer one succinct quote that speaks to this issue of relationship, but the takeaway is that (in most of Africa) a large number of very shallow relationships is actually preferred to a smaller number of deep relationships. This is because the entire purpose of having a social network is economic security. Since many people are poor, they will seek members of their social circle for financial assistance when they have a need. Everyone who is able is expected to contribute "something small." This is reciprocated each time there is a need in the "network," but these relationships are typically only financial in nature, not emotionally-driven.

There is much more that can be said about this, but an obvious conclusion for us was that developing the deep, meaningful relationships we hoped for with a people who really do not culturally engage in deep relationships, is a real struggle. Additionally, it seemed that *everyone* wanted us in their "social circle" so that they could approach us with financial needs. Again, I wish we had known this going in, because an understanding of this particular aspect of culture would have alleviated a lot of offense on our part.

Even absent this dynamic (which may be unique to Africa), the missionary life can be lonely. This challenge eventually is eliminated as sincere disciples emerge and latch on to the reality of the Kingdom life. However, a missionary going into such a situation must have enough emotional capital to endure the long, initial period of loneliness and lack of authentic fellowship. Relationships within a missionary family must go in strong. If relationships are detached or strained both inside *and* outside the home, there will be struggles on every level and it will be hard to persevere.

Another challenge is simply logistical considerations, as field service entails many major life changes; you've seen plenty of ours up to this point! Manually fetching water at a spring 900 meters from our home (for a family of ten) was a formidable task, indeed. Add the local children teasing, poking, and laughing at my children as they struggled with the unfamiliar labor, and it was as emotionally traumatic as it was physically exhausting for them. Washing laundry by hand, not having transportation, no electricity, and just acclimating to a very different life, were all part of our adjustment. There is a serious learning curve when moving across the globe. Unfortunately, there is sometimes no real preparation for these types of things. I've given my wife permission to write the next chapter, and she'll talk about some of this from a woman's perspective.

Though it's easy to say, "Learn the language and it will help you integrate and face the everyday challenges," well, there is a limit to what you can learn without being immersed in the culture. And, you learn those key phrases and make it look like you can have a conversation. But what do you do when they start talking back (really fast!) and you recognize about one word in ten? Suffice it to say, if you're planning on engaging in foreign missions, just be aware that many things will require adjustment; try to take things in stride. After four years I can now understand half of what people say, but my ability to speak is still minimal. However, I can read the Bible smoothly, since Swahili is phonetic. With sound knowledge of what verses say what, I can actually teach pretty good and fool people into thinking that I have a clue.

The dangers and risks associated with living in a developing nation will certainly strengthen your prayer life. Malaria, typhoid, yellow fever, TB, and a host of other exotic diseases are just the beginning. As hard as it is to be susceptible to these illnesses, it's equally hard dealing with the uncertainty of being sick and not being able to self-diagnose. Talk about potential hypochondria! Every fever is malaria…or is it brucellosis? Maybe typhoid? With experience comes a greater peace, but the physical aspects of living abroad can sure take their toll. Praise the Lord my family has been under His watch without significant injury. We have all had malaria multiple times, but if you diagnose and treat early enough, the effects are minimal. Me, I have malaria more often than not it seems; I have just learned to live with it, perpetually achy and tired.

In other parts of the world, there are army ants and scorpions. Thankfully, we don't need to be on watch for those. Here it's just black widows and brown recluse spiders—and lots of them—all over the house. I have been bitten by a brown recluse. It took months to heal, and I still have an ugly scar to remind me of his visit. We do have venomous snakes in our area (puff adders, black mambas, black forest cobras, rhino vipers), but we haven't personally had any problems with them.

Not much compares with the hazard of road travel. Drivers of public vehicles have little concern for safety, and the conditions of local roads don't help. Seatbelts and car seats? Ha! I have seen 27 people packed in a minivan. I personally have traveled with my wife and three children on a motorcycle. I have experienced one serious wreck, as I described elsewhere. Since then, I have been run off the road numerous times, but with no serious injuries. Our brother, Glenn, has been down on his bike about a dozen times, with many injuries, but he puts on more mileage than me. Praise God for body armor! Just go with the flow.

The potential problems on the mission field have thus far focused on some pretty practical issues associated with integrating into a new culture. There are other problems specifically related to implementing a new mission. Of course, many of those have been covered in other parts of this book as a part of other conversations. However, one thing that I really had to understand and accept as the mission chugged along was the lesson behind Jesus' teaching on the four soils.

Somehow I went into Kenya thinking that the response to the Kingdom message would be strong. After all, the gospel is for the poor, and where people do not have as many attachments to the world as we do in the West, it seems that they would respond favorably to surrendering everything and following Christ. My initial, short-term trips were also filled with accolades and positive feedback, and as I have said, I didn't realize at the time that this is a typical response to any foreigner. Thus, my expectations going in were for much greater fruitfulness than what we eventually experienced, and I had to deal with some disappointment. Yet according to Jesus, that was to be expected.

Let's look at the parable of the four soils:

> [3] And He spoke many things to them in parables, saying, "Behold, the sower went out to sow; [4] and as he sowed, some *seeds* fell beside the road, and the birds came and ate them up. [5] Others fell on the rocky places, where they did not have much soil; and immediately they sprang up, because they had no depth of soil. [6] But when the sun had risen, they were scorched; and because they had no

root, they withered away. [7] Others fell among the thorns, and the thorns came up and choked them out. [8] And others fell on the good soil and yielded a crop, some a hundredfold, some sixty, and some thirty. [9] He who has ears, let him hear.",...

[18] "Hear then the parable of the sower. [19] When anyone hears the word of the Kingdom and does not understand it, the evil *one* comes and snatches away what has been sown in his heart. This is the one on whom seed was sown beside the road. [20] The one on whom seed was sown on the rocky places, this is the man who hears the word and immediately receives it with joy; [21] yet he has no *firm* root in himself, but is *only* temporary, and when affliction or persecution arises because of the word, immediately he falls away. [22] And the one on whom seed was sown among the thorns, this is the man who hears the word, and the worry of the world and the deceitfulness of wealth choke the word, and it becomes unfruitful. [23] And the one on whom seed was sown on the good soil, this is the man who hears the word and understands it; who indeed bears fruit and brings forth, some a hundredfold, some sixty, and some thirty." (Matthew 13, see also Mark 4:3-20 and Luke 8:4-15)

Now the seed is the word of the Kingdom (Matthew 13:19). Wow, the seed is exactly what the appointed and sent ones were commanded to proclaim: the gospel of the Kingdom! People respond in one of four ways to this gospel of the Kingdom. The first group never understands the message and Satan takes away the seed that was planted. The second group receives the message, but does not endure and falls away quickly. The third likewise receives the message, and endures but does not bear fruit. Finally, the person with the good and honest heart (Luke 8:15) receives the message, understands it, and bears fruit.

According to this teaching, everyone falls into one of these categories. Our field experience perfectly validates this teaching. Some outright reject the message; we simply move on. I would say that the majority we share with actually receive the message with joy; however, that's not the end. Of those who believe, some fall away quickly because of persecution or temptation (see Luke 8:13). This group of people typically includes those who change faiths, people in forbidden relationships, and people with addictions. We of course try to restore them, but it does not always work.

The next category refers to those who persevere in believing, yet never bear fruit. As we've already seen in the context of entering the Kingdom of God and inheriting the Kingdom of God (see John 15:1-10), those who do not bear fruit will actually not inherit the Kingdom. Jesus (and others) emphasize this concept of *bearing fruit* so many times throughout the New Testament teachings (Matthew 3:7-10 and 7:15-20, Luke 13:6-9, Galatians 5:16-25), that it is essential for understanding the Kingdom of God.

In the parable of the four soils, Jesus explains why one who believes the message does not bear fruit. He states:

"[14] The *seed* which fell among the thorns, these are the ones who have heard, and as they go on their way they are choked with worries and riches and pleasures of *this* life, and bring no fruit to maturity." (Luke 8:14)

and also,

[19] but the worries of the world, and the deceitfulness of riches, and the desires for other things enter in and choke the word, and it becomes unfruitful. (Mark 4)

You can sum up fruitlessness in one word: *worldliness*. Thus, the third soil is comprised of people who love the things of the world. 1 John 2:15-17 teaches that such a person cannot have the love of the Father in him. James 4:4 says that a friend of the world is an enemy of God. So even though this third group initially looks good because they joyfully receive the message and remain for a while, they eventually return to the world and don't persevere in their faith (see 2 Peter 2:20-22).

Luke 8:15 says that the only fruit that will be born from the seed of the Kingdom gospel is in the man with a good and honest heart. Therein lies why we are instructed to seek the man of peace, and not just anyone who comes our way. Multi-generational discipleship presumes your first-generation disciple is worthy of reproduction. Absent a good and honest heart, and a willingness to count the cost and stick through to the end, they will certainly be of little use for making additional disciples. Remember, everything reproduces after its own kind. Bad trees bring forth bad fruit and good trees bring forth good fruit, and in abundance. Jesus Himself said, a disciple is not above his teacher.

If you're a leader in a pioneer mission, you'll certainly taste some successes. But oftentimes, these success story scenarios are stumbled upon through trial and error, experimenting with the opportunities presented to you by the Lord. Sometimes things work out, and other times, the "sent one" does things he would loath to replicate.

With discipleship, you are not looking for "good" people. They can be the worst of sinners. But they need an honest and good heart, such that they will earnestly confess and repent, and desire the new life in Christ. When they fail, they will be open with their weaknesses so that the brethren can counsel them and help them gain victory over their struggles. They will be willing to accept the straight-forward meaning of the Scriptures, even the hard teachings, without using mental and theological gymnastics to justify their disobedience. They will simply submit to the teachings of Christ, though it may prove difficult for them at first. They will take advice and respect those who are their elders in the faith. It does not take social status, wealth or possessions, or great intelligence to be a fruitful disciple of Christ; it just takes an honest and good heart. This is the type of disciples we want to replicate, and this is what will bear fruit.

Unfortunately, I somehow thought that I'd find something other than Jesus' 25% "success rate" in Kenya. However, our field experience has pretty well followed along with Jesus' predictions. Our East African culture is very similar to the culture in which Jesus lived and taught. We, in fact, see three in four believe and accept the word of the Kingdom. One third of those fall away quickly, and one third get caught up in worldliness eventually, even if they're around for a while. It's the one in three of the believing disciples who bears fruit from an honest and good heart.

Why is this important to understand in the mission field? Because you need to realize that this is the reality of missions; you can't let it affect your methods. Many "Kingdom" churches work hard to pre-vet prospects prior to baptism. They often go through extended periods of teaching and try to assess if the candidate is "ready" to be baptized. Yet this is not New Testament practice, nor is it in line with Jesus' clear teaching. We can't expect someone to have a real chance at bearing fruit apart from the indwelling of the Holy Spirit. Therefore, expecting "fruit" without the Spirit is completely backwards! The biblical example is that we baptize upon an individual's surrender to Christ, public confession and authentic repentance. If there are lifestyle changes required to show fruit of repentance (i.e., giving up drinking or leaving an unlawful relationship), simply verify that those changes have been made. Beyond that, there is no delaying.

The second reason why this teaching is so important is because you can get absolutely demoralized when you start to see disciples fall away, if you were not aware it is to be expected. It is, unfortunately, just the way it is. It is certainly emotionally difficult to try so hard, do everything in your power, pray without ceasing, and still see disciples make bad choices, many ultimately abandoning the faith. However, you can't take it personally. We must do *our* part and let God do *His* part. Ultimately, these prospective disciples will be accountable for their own choices.

This is one of the bigger teachings I had to make peace with, but it's not the only impediment we faced to success on the mission field. Not all missions employ indigenous people, but if you do (or plan on it), it's important to go in with your eyes open. Employing someone is similar to offering any other type of benefit, and sometimes people associate church "membership" with this. You may have people "join you" in hopes of finding a job. When the job is gone, so are they.

Then there is the unfortunate reality of having to let workers go because of poor performance or other moral issues; they, being disgruntled, will often create problems for you in the community. Of course, I regularly employ brethren so that their salary helps them find their daily bread. However, I've almost gotten to the point that I prefer hiring "outsiders" to brethren, so that there is no offense if they don't measure up to the job description and need to be let go. As well, the money can present a temptation that is too great to bear—I've seen good brothers become embittered if others get the job, or if it is only temporary.

Unfortunately, another mission-field difficulty is a little more personal and I need to be a little vague in order to protect others' privacy, but I feel compelled to address this issue nonetheless. The fact is, if you're part of a mission that involves more than you and your family, and you find yourself living in any type of community with other missionaries, *you can expect conflicts*. To assume everything will go smoothly just because you're all Christians is simply naïve.

We have had our share of ups and downs with other missionaries who served alongside of us, and I'll repeat what someone wise once told me: "There are three sides to every story: yours, theirs, and the truth." Even as Christians, we all have baggage. We view things through a certain lens and react in ways that other people may not expect or understand. Personalities vary greatly! Yet our unity is vital to keeping the mission on-track. Missionaries are under a microscope and there really is no easy way to explain to sincere, indigenous disciples why there are problems between folks who are living and serving together.

If you find yourself experiencing relationship difficulties with others in the field, my best advice is the same I offer in many other situations: *obey Jesus*. Look at how He told us to address conflicts in Matthew 18. Do it. Don't be afraid to express yourself, with gentleness and respect, with a brother. Don't gossip about or slander a brother, *talk directly to him* until the issue is worked out. If you don't feel you can, just pray. God can do things in others that we cannot force by our own actions. In the meantime, follow the way of love that we read about in 1 Corinthians 13. Don't keep a record of wrongs. Be willing to overlook offenses. Focus on what is positive in those with whom you serve. As Jesus advised, turn the other cheek. As Paul recommended, "in humility, consider others better than yourself" (Philippians 2:3). Seek peace and pursue it! The Scriptures are not silent on inter-personal relationships and how we should respond to others; however, when things are hard, it is all too easy to stumble.

In situations where there is conflict, there is rarely just one person in the wrong; we all behave and respond wrongly at times, and often one person's negative actions fuel an equally negative reaction. As God's holy people, we should be above this, but unfortunately, *we're not*. Humility is important in acknowledging our part in conflicts, if we're going to get beyond them. We all have our weaknesses, and not every character flaw is an unforgiveable sin. People who have a mutual commitment to each other will persevere through hard things, and if they do, they will experience joy and deeper fellowship on the other side. Finding peace in conflict does take time, however, and we often need to be patient as we wait on God and others for change.

In our mission field experience, we've certainly had our share of conflicts between the various workers. Unfortunately, we did not always work them out in a God-honoring way, and we've experienced negative effects as a result. Communication between parties at all phases of integration into the mission, and while working together, is a vital necessity if conflict is to be mitigated. Otherwise our four-phase pioneer mission will never reach sustainability and reproducibility.

Chapter 11: A Woman's Perspective

Written by Cindy Carrier

As the last chapter suggests, and the rest of our story spells out pretty well, moving a large family half-way across the world to participate in an as-yet undefined mission with little support on the ground, is quite an adventure. I've already written about how we dealt with some of the issues surrounding the move and integrating into a new culture in my book, *The Kingdom of God is not about Eating and Drinking*. However, Marc thought that a woman's perspective would be helpful here for those "sent ones" who aren't going alone to their pioneer missions.

The apostle Paul was right—a single person being sent out certainly can devote him or herself to the Lord in an unhindered way, whereas a family man has divided interests. Going in to Kenya, Marc and I both were committed to settling where the Lord called us, but we did have interest in maintaining some kind of security and continuity for the children. We might have been content with a thatched-roof mud hut, but largely because of the children, we opted for brick and mortar. Other considerations were likewise made with the children in mind, both in anticipation of the move and during our time abroad.

One simple example: in our second year, the children received gift money for Christmas from their grandfather. He asked us to get them something they really wanted. Their near-unanimous decision? Bicycles! As parents, of course we wanted to give our children this good thing. Yet in our small village, children's bicycles are unheard of. They can be bought in the next big town, but they are expensive and certainly would set us apart from the community in a major way, which was totally opposite our overall goal. We had eight children and could get away with getting five bikes of different sizes to be shared amongst all the children. But—five bikes?! Yet, the children had willingly left behind their bikes in America and had little else of their own in Kenya for entertainment and of course, exercise. It was a small concession, but it seemed like such a big thing.

The children were aware of our vacillating thoughts regarding purchasing bikes. Though they wanted them, they expressed willingness to do whatever we felt best, which they knew would be whatever was best for the mission. In the end, we agreed to the bike purchase. I think it did affect the children's relationships with other kids in the community somewhat, as they later confessed that they felt like people didn't really want to be their friends, but rather just came over to swing on our swing set or ride bikes. I'm not sure if knowing the outcome would have changed their decision, but this is just one example of a day-to-day decision that might be easily made stateside, yet is exponentially more difficult on the mission field. There are many like this, most revolving around the use of money and the appearance of wealth.

However, many of the day-to-day events and issues our family faces on the mission field don't differ much from our stateside life. I'm still homeschooling, managing the home, and supporting my husband in various practical ways. We still try to build family relationships, I mediate conflicts between children, and we look for ways to serve one another and our community. Whether on the mission field or off, when I am asked, "So what do you do?" the answer revolves around all the things that younger women are encouraged to do in Titus 2:4-5:

> to love their husbands, to love their children, [5] *to be* sensible, pure, workers at home, kind, being subject to their own husbands, so that the word of God will not be dishonored.

When we first moved to Kenya, dealing with the culture shock and sudden manual labor occupied most of our time and energy. During this season, "loving my husband" meant cheerfully adapting to hand-washing laundry, encouraging the children to have good attitudes about things like hauling water multiple times each day so that the home atmosphere remained positive, and sitting down with the constant influx of visitors to serve *chai* and make small talk.

Of course, sometimes all this was easier said than done. During rainy season when my clothes just *would not dry*, I had a fighting chance of getting enough sun if only I could start the laundry at about 6:30 and have it hung out by 8:00. But that desire was usually dashed by the need to get breakfast on the table, or the nine month-old baby who wanted to nurse, or making sure the children got organized to dress, brush their hair, and head out to fetch water. By the time breakfast was done and I could finally start laundry, I'd often have to interrupt the task to entertain visitors. This was no small frustration, of course, but it was part of my husband's "job description," and therefore my job was to help.

During those early days, emotions were often raw as we all struggled to acclimate to this radically new place. We missed many of the comforts and conveniences, and just the familiarity, of home. But Kenya now *was* home. "Loving my children" sometimes meant finding ways to connect with them in spite of the sudden onslaught of hard work that we all tried to shoulder together. At other times, loving them was "tough love" as I encouraged them out of bad attitudes with Bible verses like, "Whatever you do, work at it with all your heart as working for the Lord!" Most days, *loving* was just constantly *serving*, and I wondered if that was enough to keep our relationships solid.

In line with Titus 2:5, there was certainly no shortage of work to do at home! At that time, our oldest son was 12, down to our youngest, who was only 9 months. While the four oldest children were pretty capable at helping with work around the house, much of it now was done in a much different way than what they were used to. During this learning curve, I (of course) had to pick up most of the slack. Not to mention, their task of fetching water each morning took so much time that by the time our indoor tank was filled for the day, the children needed to be starting school, anyway. So for me to stay busy at home was really *no problem.*

The conflict arose once we started making connections in the community, and several of the women I began talking with regularly wanted me to share the Kingdom with people that they knew. Though many attended church, this "Gospel of the Kingdom" was new to them, and I was actually excited by the opportunity to get out and be about the Lord's business, since it seemed a door was opening for that. However, as I began to spend two and sometimes three mornings each week out and about, our home management, and the children's attitudes, began to suffer. There just didn't seem to be enough hours in the day to get everything done. I'd ask the children to pick up the slack if I was going to be away, and if I came home to disarray and chaos, I admit, I didn't have the best reaction. As well, I had to take the nursing baby with me, and he didn't exactly have the most cooperative temperament. The long walks to various locations and extended meetings that *never* started on time were filled with much stress as I tried to accommodate an unhappy baby.

Feeling like this was what God wanted me to be doing, I struggled through many months of this routine. Finally, at the breaking point, I asked Marc, "Should I really be going to all these meetings? I feel like I'm neglecting things at home, yet I don't want to stop doing what God wants me to do!" The question was, was it what God wanted, or simply what the people around me expected? After much soul-searching and discussion, we determined that I should step back and re-focus on home and family.

During our second year, things normalized somewhat. We decided to hire a neighbor to do our daily wash, freeing me up to spend more time homeschooling (which I felt was being neglected). At this point, indoor running water and a solar system were added blessings that alleviated much home management stress and labor. As well, spending more time at home bore fruit in improved relationships and inter-personal interactions. Not the least, my little baby was maturing and becoming much more independent.

At that time, the initial focus on evangelism in the ministry turned to discipleship. Due to the number of people who had been added to our fellowships, Marc was continually inviting small groups of people over for specific teachings or just discussion. During this season, my support role meant having an "open door" policy (meaning the house had to always be neat), putting on pots of *chai*, scraping together afternoon snacks, and often making lots of extra lunch, in the event that unexpected visitors showed up (which they often did).

During every season of our life in Kenya, we've also hosted many indigenous and *wazungu* visitors: leaders or members from far-away fellowships, fellow missionaries from other parts of Kenya, short-term missionaries from America, and donors to the ongoing work of Kingdom Driven Ministries. These visits have usually been a blessing in the fellowship they offer, but they do add a significant amount of work to the day: setting up rooms, cooking extra food and washing extra clothes and dishes, taking extra care with home management, heating up water for many more evening baths, and sometimes, just keeping the kids in a new routine and *quiet* at times!

As we integrated lots of women into our fellowship, I began teaching a weekly women's Bible study. This was different from the initial meetings I went to, as they were local and usually included a core group of women. I also set the start time myself, and tried to stick to it. Thus, this weekly event really didn't put too much stress on me or on the home. I really enjoyed being with the women, encouraging them, and getting to know them.

We also began getting lots of medical needs brought to our attention, so I often found my day interrupted for bandaging wounds, washing various kinds of infestations, or giving away medicine from our store of cough medicine, malaria tablets, and ibuprofen. I was happy for this opportunity to serve, though I often felt in over my head and a little insecure about being viewed as having any significant medical knowledge.

Another joy was being able to greet and chat with people who came for food assistance. We kept bags of maize, beans, and rice (in our bedroom, the only available space!), so that when folks came we could put together small packages for them. My older girls often helped with this and I appreciated that we could all serve as a family to meet needs in our community. For some reason, I developed a special connection with a woman named Sharon. We couldn't communicate very well, of course, but we both tried. I mostly liked her smile and her humble demeanor. After several times of her coming for both food and medicine, I learned that she had been abandoned by her husband and had several small children at home. I always added soap, fruit if I had it, and some extra goodies to her basic food package.

A weekly responsibility that I took on for a time was to host communion in our home, which meant setting up seating and making rice and beans with *chai* for as many as 25 people. I would make a single *chapati* (flat bread) and buy a bottle of cheap fruit juice from Titus's shop for communion. At times I'd forget to fill the basins of water and put out the towel for foot washing, but our visitors were gracious and went with the flow. Those times of celebrating church ordinances in our home were precious to me, and something I miss now that we have a separate meeting room for such gatherings. As we sometimes struggled to communicate, I would find myself thinking ahead to that time when we—how many of us, and which of us?—would be together in the eternal Kingdom, praising our King together with no barriers of separation!

During our third year, the medical and food needs seemed to increase and I was spending more and more time interrupting our daily routines to serve whoever came to the door. Though it sometimes felt burdensome, I knew that this was how God wanted me to support my husband and serve Him during this season. The *mzungu* family that moved into our compound that year included an older woman who eventually expressed interest in taking charge of the ongoing women's discipleship group. She was also now responsible for the medical needs that I had previously been taking care of. All in all, this delegation of responsibility felt like a breath of fresh air.

Of course, there were still impromptu visitors and monthly or bi-monthly "all church" teaching sessions on Saturdays, which included morning *chai* and afternoon lunch for anywhere between 10 and 25 people. That meant clearing, sweeping, and mopping our veranda, setting up chairs, and putting out the water filter early in the morning, and then getting right to work on lunch preparation! My "meals for a crowd" menu varied, depending on time constraints and what I had on hand, but usually included rice and beans or *githeri* (boiled rice and maize, a common lunch here). Though each day seemed to be filled to its fullest, I often spoke aloud what now seemed to be my life verse: "...whoever serves *is to do so* as one who is serving by the strength which God supplies; so that in all things God may be glorified through Jesus Christ, to whom belongs the glory and dominion forever and ever. Amen." (1 Peter 4:11)

At the time of this writing, we're now entering our fifth year here in Kenya. At this point, we're in the transitional phase of raising up indigenous leaders, so we're trying to get our hands off of many things and give the churches independence. Much of my previous work and service is being done by others. On one hand, it's somewhat of a relief. I am able to re-focus on my own family and on homeschooling, which again seems to have fallen by the wayside in some areas. On the other hand, I miss being so intimately involved with the ministry and with people. In this season, I am supporting my husband and the mission by writing reports, editing and posting blog entries written by one of our African brothers, and doing whatever else (usually administrative in nature) is needed.

However, we're on the cusp of moving to Uganda permanently, as our house is under construction and a new mission has already been launched. (More on that in the next chapter.) I anticipate that, with the move, I'll be repeating much of what we went through during our first years here: doing a lot of work manually, entertaining visitors, building relationships, being involved in women's discipleship. I look forward with anticipation to what the Lord has in store for our family on this second phase of our great adventure on-mission in East Africa.

Throughout these years, I have often thought of the apostle Paul's question, "Do we not have a right to take along a believing wife, even as the rest of the apostles and the brothers of the Lord and Cephas?" (1 Corinthians 9:5). I've wondered, just what *is* the role of "a believing wife" on the mission? The Scriptures are pretty silent on the subject. But I think it has a lot to do with staying focused on those Titus 2:4-5 commands to young women: loving their husbands and children, managing the home, being kind (serving others), and being subject to their husbands. My role, in other words, entails meeting practical needs in the home, and doing whatever is needed to support my husband's work and the work of the Kingdom, day-by-day. Each day, each season, the demands are different, but the over-arching goal is the same: to glorify God by being obedient to His Word.

Marc has said how important it is to make sure your family life is in order before you take off for a foreign mission field. I couldn't agree more! There are so many stresses associated with serving the Lord abroad, that if there is not a solid foundation, family members will find themselves at odds with each other. This will only complicate whatever work the Lord has called you to do. It's important to be cognizant of relationships throughout every phase of life on-mission and proactively address potential problems.

For example, one of our children has a very hard time accepting change. I was careful to discuss every step of the move with this child in detail, going over just what could be expected, what the response should be to various possible outcomes, and so on—with plenty advance notice so they could get used to the idea of the "new normal." For a child with difficulty adjusting, you can expect problems if you allow life to just happen and assume they will "go with the flow."

During the transition, we all needed to give each other lots of grace, as our actions and re-actions to so many changes were not always optimal. Marc and I were quick to apologize to the children (and each other) if we were irritable or responded inappropriately, and we encouraged the children to "be quick to listen, slow to speak, and slow to become angry" with each other. I wore out many Bible verses (spoken in gentle tones) in dealing with their complaining about the overload of manual labor, as I wanted to nip it in the bud without nagging. I also tried to be enthusiastic about the changes and even the challenges. Even if I felt like I was "faking it" at times, it helped us all have a better overall attitude.

I've shared some of the ways I've been able to support Marc's work on the mission field, and perhaps you have some idea of what the work of the ministry has added to my plate. Personally, I've also had to struggle through some issues, which only added to the occasional sense of burden.

The first such adjustment was being totally home-bound during our first year and a half with no vehicle. (How do you go anywhere when you have eight children and the only available mode of transportation is a motorbike? You don't!) The only exception was the various meetings I walked to, which I really didn't consider "enjoyable." This represents a significant loss of independence, as in America I was used to jumping into our 15-passenger van at will and going shopping, to the park, to the library, to the museum, or to a friend's. Even though we now have a car, I still don't drive. But I do enjoy running errands in town and going out to lunch with my husband on occasion.

I was also initially bothered by the constant illnesses and my relative inability to diagnose or treat them: amoeba from water, giardia, seasonal allergies, MRSA boils, malaria. After our first year (and with the introduction of our own well and indoor water), many of the water-borne issues were alleviated—praise the Lord! We also learned to identify other illnesses early on and kept certain medicines *always* on the shelf. Slowly but surely, I adapted to this significant stressor as well.

In our early years of marriage with many young children, I had often battled depression but, with the help of the Lord, had experienced much victory in the area of emotions. Even so, coming to Kenya with a nursing nine month-old, I found myself battling hormonal fluctuations at times. This never helped on those difficult days, but God's grace, constant prayer, and positive self-talk helped me get through any rough moments. During our third and fourth years in Kenya, I experienced four miscarriages; although these were emotional times I also knew I could trust in the sovereignty of God. Our ninth child, born at home with the help of a nurse from the local clinic, was a true blessing when she arrived!

Elsewhere, Marc has shared about the importance of having a definite call from the Lord if you are serving on the mission field. Absent such clarity, it would be easy to give up when challenges arise. While the call is my husband's, God has also confirmed my support of him in this work. I'll admit to thinking many times, "I want to go home!," but those have truly been fleeting thoughts. During one of those moments, I stumbled across a quote from John Piper that really resonated with me:

> Occasionally weep deeply over the life you hoped would be. Grieve the losses. Then wash your face. Trust God. And embrace the life you have.

This describes fairly accurately how I have operated during hard times. After indulging in some tears, feelings of homesickness, or thoughts of what "could be," I shift my thoughts back to what is, and press on. I truly embrace the life we have. Although I'm not an apostle, I suppose I would classify myself as a capable helpmeet. As members of one body, each of us plays a part; as a family, we have been able to contribute to implementing a sustainable reproducible mission, and for that I give thanks to God.

Chapter 12: New Pioneer Mission Launched!

In case it hasn't been obvious up to this point, no matter how well-prepared I thought I was to be a pioneer missionary, a lot of things just had to be learned from experience. Every "sent one" likely gets surprised by circumstances sometimes, and just has to go with the flow. Yet the time came when the four-phase mission was implemented with regularity in various locations, and the experience for the disciples was predictable and consistent.

My second-generation leaders hadn't formally graduated to managing the mission on their own, but I knew they'd be ready soon. In the MAWL paradigm, we could safely enter the *"watch"* phase before final let-go. But there is a lot to release! A sustainable, reproducible mission will focus on all the following elements in discipleship and leadership development:

- Evangelism and evangelism training
- Reading and teaching the Bible
- Guiding someone through repentance
- Instructions on baptism
- Facilitating Communion
- Church discipline
- Prayer and fasting
- Ministering to the needs of others
- Performing marriages and burials
- Leadership development
- Leadership appointment

Much had been invested during our third and fourth years in these various elements of leadership development. Now that we were nearing hand-off on the Kenya mission, I began to pray about what was next. I knew that having an exit strategy for the mission was a must, but where would I go? What would I do? I spent time in thought and prayer, talked to the family, and strategized with key mission leaders. Eventually, we decided that Uganda was the place. I let my indigenous apostle-in-training, Timothy, visit a couple locations just across the border from Kenya (along with a second person) to see what the response would be to the Kingdom message. If it was favorable, I would take that as an indication to press forward with a more permanent move.

As this part of the plan got underway and we watched to see how things unfolded, I found a partner with whom I could file my Uganda work permit. The family and I had to stay in Uganda for several weeks while our passports were stamped and everything was approved for our long-term stay. Even so, we weren't ready for a permanent move yet, as the Lord had not revealed where we would live.

We visited Uganda with one of our Kenyan ordained evangelists, who had a family history among a specific tribe in Uganda. In two-by-two fashion, we visited several potential locations and favored one in particular. However, each of the exploratory visits by Timothy eventually encountered roadblocks of different kinds, so in the end, the Lord's direction was obvious. We would press forward at the location we had visited.

Our house construction wasn't without troubles, of course. We tried to apply many of the lessons we had learned in Kenya, so I'd say it went as good as it possibly could have. The pioneer mission, on the other hand, went better than expected. We didn't wait until we were resident to find our man of peace and get the ball rolling; instead, a Kenyan disciple and I started the process while we were in-country. Not finding a man of peace at that time (we talked to two people who had potential, but didn't receive the teachings in the end), he later returned (with my 17 year-old son as a second person) while house construction was underway. It was my desire to "minimize the *mzungu*" as much as possible on the new mission front, in hopes of avoiding some of the pitfalls of the original Kenya mission.

My son (who is fluent in Swahili) and our Kenyan brother spent extensive time interacting with the local population as they supervised the house construction. After some time and prayer, one man emerged as having a good and honest heart, and exhibited much humility. The evangelists were invited to his home to preach the Kingdom; this man of peace had organized 24 people to hear the message! As many as ten were very interested and asked for more teaching.

A few days later, the smaller group was prepared to hear deeper teachings about surrendering to Christ, repentance and baptism. Ultimately, five surrendered, repented, and were baptized. The evangelists returned to teach the commands of Christ (our book three) in the next session. Following that teaching, two hold-outs from the prior session surrendered, repented and were baptized as well. The fledgling fellowship now boasted seven new Kingdom disciples. The evangelists proceeded to teach them what the Scriptures said about church, and how to execute a Discovery Bible Study (DBS).

Once teachings started in this location, many people got wind of the goings-on and wanted to join mid-stream. However, the vigilant evangelists would not permit it. Only those who had been taught the Kingdom gospel were permitted to learn about surrender, repentance and baptism. Only those present in the second session attended the third session. You get the drift. The hopefuls were told they would simply have to wait their turn. Why, you ask? If they had allowed late-comers to join the group, yet pressed on with the advanced teaching, the late-joining group would be left with significant gaps in understanding. If teaching started over from the beginning with both groups together, there's no guarantee that the original folks wouldn't lose interest with the re-teaching. When this happens (and it often does), it's usually best to stick with the original group until the foundations are in place, and then those folks can participate in the teaching of a second group, if desired. Great on-the-job training! Patience is key—go slow in order to go fast, and finish what you start.

Of course, what we learned in Kenya will undoubtedly prove true in Uganda as well: in every group of those who receive the Kingdom through surrender, repentance, and baptism, only one of three will persevere unto fruitfulness, no matter what it looks like in the beginning. So when I share our Uganda success story, well, I know it isn't over yet. Even so, a movement that has the potential to multiply has been set in motion.

Here is a quote from Nik Ripken's *The Insanity of Obedience*, about the Chinese house church movement (the fastest-growing advancement of the Kingdom the world has ever seen):

> Recently, we led a training meeting with some believers in China. In public remarks, I commented on the significant spiritual harvest among the Chinese. I enthusiastically described how that harvest had been an encouragement to the global Body of Christ. ...
>
> After my remarks, a Chinese house church leader asked me to join him for a meal. With unflagging gentleness, this church leader firmly challenged the number of believers in China that I had cited. His comment took me off guard; after all, I had used the most conservative estimate quoted by Westerners! I defended my figures and I explained to my host the source of my statistics. He listened to me patiently. Then, with a smile, he agreed it might be possible to support the numbers which I was using. At the same time, he suggested a different way of interpreting the numbers being bandied globally.
>
> I will never forget what he said next: 'Of that large number of believers that you described in your talk, two-thirds of those people are what we would call "members." Only one-third of those people are who we would call "true followers of Jesus.'
>
> I was puzzled by that distinction and I asked my new friend to explain the difference in these two categories.
>
> He said, "Probably two-thirds of the people you mentioned regularly attend a house church. Most of those people have been baptized. Most of the people contribute financially to the work of a house church." He paused before continuing: "*But we do not consider church members to be true followers of Jesus until they have led other people to Christ and until they have helped plant more house churches.*"

Note that the one-in-three trend of fruitfulness is not unique to our mission, as one would anticipate since Jesus Himself made clear this was to be expected in His parable of the four soils. Also note the huge philosophical disconnect between the Western understanding of the role of a disciple, and the Chinese understanding. *Reproduction* is in their DNA, while *membership* typically is in ours. Their churches are apostolic by design and execution, and outwardly focused on expansion. Western churches are predominantly pastoral, and inwardly focused on keeping congregants. Remember, God is in charge, and his goal is to serve a four-phase mission to His disciples: evangelism, discipleship, church development, and the Great Commandment—in an unending cycle that is sustainable and reproducible. Let's not lose this focus!

On the topic of the Chinese house church is a subject that has not yet come up here, because our Kenya mission is very much taking place in a "post-Christian" environment: *persecution*. While many missionaries (or even people at home in the West) don't run towards persecution, honestly, it's potentially one of the greatest assets in promulgating a sustainable and reproducible Kingdom mission. Under heavy persecution, leadership development is a very high priority; the churches must be ready at any given time for their leadership to be arrested or killed, necessitating the next-generation disciples to quickly fill the vacuum. Not only that, the disciples themselves, knowing the risks of professing faith in Christ, are less likely to make a commitment that is insincere.

Peacetime and security lead to complacency; there is little sense of urgency in a post-Christian ministry. I believe every single appointed and sent one needs to leverage the benefits of living under persecution, even while living in safety. In other words, they should design and execute their mission *as if* they were going to imminently depart. In fact, their departure should be part of their plan. *Having an exit strategy is vitally important to prepare a mission for sustainability and reproducibility.*

Transitioning to Uganda was a chance for me to start something new, but I still need to exit Kenya. We are well on our way to having a self-governing and self-sustaining body of believers in Kenya, but some leadership positions are in limbo and some "watching" is still needed before I would assert that the church is ready to stand on its own.

This is what Paul told Timothy: "The things which you have heard from me in the presence of many witnesses, entrust these to faithful men who will be able to teach others also" (2 Timothy 2:2). This is multi-generational discipleship. Paul taught Timothy, who would then teach "faithful men," who would "teach others." Focusing on multi-generational discipleship and leadership development ensures the longevity of the mission. I knew this going in, and after four long years, most of the pieces are finally in place.

Each location and culture will face various challenges once the time comes for churches to exercise their independence. Will the church in Kenya continue the processes of evangelism, discipleship, church development, and Great Commandment works on its own? Will the individual fellowships stand or fall? Though I cannot say for sure which way the pendulum will swing for the existing fellowships that have resulted from our Kenya mission, I can say with confidence that I have followed the apostolic pattern to the best of my ability and have done everything in my power to ensure that a sustainable, reproducible movement has been set in motion. As with all matters related to our faith, there is an element of personal choice, and we have an enemy who will work against Kingdom expansion.

As mentioned previously, the foundation of Christ is laid by the apostles and prophets, and those who build on that foundation will be accountable for their work. I believe that the quality of the work will not be evident until the churches are required to stand on their own. Thus, as to the success or failure of any pioneer mission, only time will tell.

Chapter 13: The Role of Heavenly Investors

When an entrepreneur wants to start a new enterprise, he's going to need investors. Those investor relations are vitally important, and they will expect a return—the more, the better. If, in our analogy, God Himself is the one in charge of choosing the people who work in the places He has in mind, then the investors are those Christians who respond to the financial needs and enable the work to be done. And the return on investment is out of this world! When you give to God's work, you're storing up for yourselves treasures in Heaven (see Matthew 6:2-4, 19-21).

There's no enterprise without an owner backing it, and it won't succeed without a capable leader on staff; however, absent a financial injection (particularly before the enterprise opens and becomes successful in its own right), the endeavor will be over before it started. In the same way, I would argue that (apart from God Himself), ministry partners are one of the most vital participants in the mission enterprise. They give financially, which is important. But just as necessary is their personal investment in the work of the Lord that leads them to consistently keep the mission and its needs in prayer. As one of my mentors said, "Five hours of prayer yields five minutes of power!"

One of our greatest challenges through the years has been maintaining connection with our partners. Since we have been so busy doing the work, we rarely have had sufficient time to sit down and write about the work we are doing. (And a terrible Internet connection certainly doesn't help!) Yet the lifeblood of our pioneer mission operations is our ministry partners.

Even if you are baptizing and helping thousands of people, if no one knows about it, support will dry up almost immediately and you won't be able to continue the work. Faithful partners are nurtured through regular communication. They must buy into the vision and mission if they are going to invest their hard-earned money and sacrifice time to pray for the work. If you are on the mission field (or plan to be), make time for regular email updates, prayer requests, Facebook posts, blogs and newsletter, private messages, and simply real conversation. In these days of technological innovation and connectedness, you have many venues available to stay connected—do it! Do not take for granted that the Lord's work, in which you are privileged to participate, is a team effort. Your financial and prayer partners help make what you do successful.

One word of caution: many great-hearted people out there have "pet" passions that may not sync with your core mission. It will be a great temptation to participate in projects outside of your vision and mission simply because the funding is there, and people may want to do the work. Think about it according to this analogy: the owner of the enterprise has a vision and is the one in charge of how the plans unfold. If he allows investors to be a part of his Board of Directors, perhaps they'll have some input on operations; if not, they simply get a financial return based on what the owner does with his location, staff, and personal vision. A mission is the Lord's work, not ours. We are all players on the team and have to follow the same vision, or it's possible to be sidetracked—even derailed—in the work of the ministry.

These temptations to get sidetracked from the core mission are real and may be very attractive for a variety of reasons. But I'll be honest, if you allow yourself to be driven by funding, you're a slave to Mammon, not to Christ. We've allowed ourselves to get distracted by a couple projects that were outside our core mission, and we regretted it every time. These projects have nearly always resulted in a disruption to discipleship and Kingdom expansion at some level.

We recently read "The Heavenly Man," the story of Brother Yun, a man who was "sent" to his own people in China with the message of Jesus. In spite of (or perhaps, because of) years of persecution, the Chinese church was strong and unified. That is, until Western benefactors began to assist the fellowships in various ways. I thought it might be instructive to share Brother Yun's thoughts here:

> After a while our foreign friends started giving even more things to us. They gave money, cameras, and other things they felt were necessary to help us serve the Lord more effectively. I clearly remember how this caused division among the leaders. In our evil hearts we asked, "Who got the most books?" or, "Why was that brother given more money than me?" It was a real mess. Within a year or two, the house churches in China split into ten or twelve fragments. This was how so many different house church networks came into existence.

> It was easy for a house church to split. Sometimes an outsider would come and spend time with a group of second or third-level leaders. They would hand out "support" money and their contact cards. Within a short time a new movement would be established. In their zeal to help, our foreign brothers were actually causing the house churches to split and be weakened. ...

> [T]he motive in giving and receiving must be pure, and these gifts should only be given through the existing church leadership, so that younger leaders are not tempted to use these gifts to usurp the authority of the leaders above them.

These words are directed toward both potential donors and recipients, and I think the lessons we can learn are clear. Those who receive should not compare the gifts they get to others around them, with a spirit of covetousness that will lead to division. And those who give, need to be careful to do so in thoughtful ways and according to the leadership structure that is already in place.

Most of the thoughts in this section are directed toward the sent one who is a vision-bearer of the mission God has asked him to participate in. However, I'm sure some KDM donors will, at some point, pick up this book. We want you to know just how much we value your partnership! Hopefully, as you've seen the mission unfold in the pages of this book, you can see the fruit born from your investment. Just in case you're not entirely familiar with what we have done and are doing as a mission, allow me to share not only the "what" but the "why."

Our medical assistance program is designed to help with acute medical emergencies where people can't afford treatment. We do not address chronic conditions where there are ongoing needs, unless we make a special solicitation. These are done on a case-by-case basis. Our malnutrition program provides sufficient nutritional supplementation to facilitate proper development during children's critical early years. Our HIV program simply ensures that those infected have access to their government-provided medication. (We provide transport to and from the District Hospital, where free medicine is made available on a monthly basis.)

We also provide food, in the form of the local staple here, maize, to all who need it; yet, we limit the amount to only one kilogram per week. We want the food to function as a supplement, providing for a real need and yet encouraging people to continue to struggle in earning their "daily bread."

Another function of KDM, which we did not necessarily anticipate at first but which became evident as a need, is to help with the burials of deceased disciples. Given that this is a large expense (and might be a motivating reason for people to "join" our church), how do we do this in a way that is sustainable and does not present a temptation for perceived financial gain? We decided that we would not have a policy to help financially with burials, or offer a certain "guaranteed" amount of assistance; however, if the need arose, we would write up a report and solicit for donations that would be earmarked. Thus, when people come to us with a burial need, we always tell them, "We can try…and you can pray!" Glory to God, He has always come through to meet the majority of such requests.

At this point in the Kenya mission, all "Great Commandment" work is now done at an independent office location. A church-appointed deacon administers all of our various programs with the assistance of other disciples. We have fixed budgets which were developed based on evaluating average expenses, and we have donors who support these programs. The monthly budget amount is given to the deacon on the first of every month. He purchases and distributes all supplies and provides for all medical needs, maintaining very detailed accounts with all receipts. All needs are directed to Africans and met by Africans.

Our deacon attends to all routine medical cases. He sees the patient and makes a very superficial assessment, confirming that the case meets our treatment criteria. If treatment is approved, he stamps a slip with our official seal, and sends the patient to a local clinic with a list of symptoms. We have an arrangement with this clinic that they keep an account for us (a very unusual arrangement here in Africa!). Twice monthly, our deacon goes to the clinic and pays the bill. If the local clinic refers the patient to another hospital, we send two trusted disciples with the patient to see to it they receive care. These escorts always travel two-by-two for accountability, and because travel can be risky.

For special cases, one of our African brothers photographs the patient and writes a brief report so that we can solicit funding for the case. We only proceed with these cases if our donors are compelled to contribute towards the need. We do not have means to proceed otherwise. In this way, we feel it is in the Lord's hands and it encourages much prayer by the disciples and the patients.

So what is the role of donors in a foreign mission? Frankly getting a mission off the ground in the modern world is not free. Housing, permitting, and air travel alone are huge expenses. Though we self-funded these expenses for our first pioneer mission, repeating the process in new pioneer fields can prove too costly for low-income foreign workers, so an initial investment to set the mission in motion is usually necessary. A long-term missionary who is unable to work on the mission field or who is not self-supported may need ongoing assistance. However, I would contend that a long-term missionary (in most cases) should not have an extended commitment to one area, but should pioneer new sites once others have proven their ability to self-govern.

Financial partners in the mission are likewise given an opportunity to meet a myriad of vital needs among the poor in developing nations (these needs will vary, depending on the focus and location of the mission). However, as an associate of mine wisely noted, medical needs in particular are almost never-ending in developing nations. It is not practical to assume that such programs will necessarily continue once the long-term missionary exits. An exit strategy may provide for ongoing charitable work; however, it would ideally be self-sustaining in some way.

This book's emphasis on developing a sustainable, reproducible mission should not, at this point, be misunderstood. It refers to the ongoing evangelism, discipleship, church development, and Great Commandment processes that should be self-replicating, even in the absence of the initiating missionary. This does not mean that any programs that have been put in place through the financial assistance of outsiders is necessarily self-replicating. Each of these processes should, in fact, not be dependent on outside funding. Even Great Commandment works are ideally person-to-person, according to ability, and not organizational in nature.

We see in Scripture that Paul and Silas, with help from Titus, took up a collection from the more affluent churches to assist the saints who were enduring a famine:

> [3] For I testify that according to their ability, and beyond their ability, *they gave* of their own accord, [4] begging us with much urging for the favor of participation in the support of the saints, [5] and *this*, not as we had expected, but they first gave themselves to the Lord and to us by the will of God. (2 Corinthians 8)

Paul explains the "rules of engagement" in this matter of giving: the collection was made specifically so that the more affluent churches could assist the poorer saints in their affliction. This was a special offering for an emergency, not ongoing upkeep. Under normal circumstances, local churches met their own needs. Paul further expresses the goal of giving:

> [7] But just as you abound in everything, in faith and utterance and knowledge and in all earnestness and in the love we inspired in you, *see* that you abound in this gracious work also. [8] I am not speaking *this* as a command, but as proving through the earnestness of others the sincerity of your love also. [9] For you know the grace of our Lord Jesus Christ, that though He was rich, yet for your sake He became poor, so that you through His poverty might become rich. [10] I give *my* opinion in this matter, for this is to your advantage, who were the first to begin a year ago not only to do *this*, but also to desire *to do it*. [11] But now finish doing it also, so that just as *there was* the readiness to desire it, so *there may be* also the completion of it by your ability. [12] For if the readiness is present, it is acceptable according to what *a person* has, not according to what he does not have. [13] For *this* is not for the ease of others *and* for your affliction, but by way of equality— [14] at this present time your abundance *being a supply* for their need, so that their abundance also may become *a supply* for your need, that there may be equality; [15] as it is written, "HE WHO *gathered* MUCH DID NOT HAVE TOO MUCH, AND HE WHO *gathered* LITTLE HAD NO LACK." (2 Corinthians 8)

Those who have, give from what they have to assist those who lack, *that there might be equality*. This collection was in response to a regional famine. That means it was a disaster that overwhelmed the existing infrastructure such that they could not meet their own needs (though under normal circumstances they were expected to do so). The gift was for necessities (food). It was collected and delivered by the apostles and though not specified, was undoubtedly administered by the deacons. This is precisely how KDM has designed, and executes, the African mission: making collections for needs and asking Kingdom brethren from around the world to participate in the work, that there might be equality.

However, we do expect local churches to meet their own needs under normal circumstances. Keep in mind that the people in East Africa been living here forever—working, feeding themselves, marrying and burying, for countless generations. Absent some disaster, the people have developed an infrastructure to meet life's needs. *Westerners should not look at the primitive lifestyles of a developing country and assume that people are somehow disadvantaged due to the simplicity of their lives.* I personally believe that they have a great advantage and do not wish modernity on anyone. The "thorns and thistles" are best left in the West. Let them live in dignity without interfering with their lives, apart from assisting with absolute necessities or disaster relief.

Through the pages of this book, you've seen what has been accomplished through Kingdom Driven Ministries...but where are we going from here? Kenya.

Tanzania. Uganda. …and from there, the Lord will order our steps. We've gone from one disciple, to numerous churches, and now, to numerous nations. Our indigenous disciples are training our future leaders. Our first mission front is very near self-sustaining. It is time to repeat the process, again and again. The harvest is ready, but the laborers are few.

I had a dream somewhat recently that a single well-wisher donated a very large sum of money to Kingdom Driven Ministries. I woke up and pondered, "What would I change if money were no object?" It was a real valuable exercise. In the end, I decided I would not change much at all concerning the core mission; really, just some small things that could make a big difference. But then I did consider new things I would certainly do if money were no object, all concerning "beseeching the Lord of the harvest to send out more laborers."

We want hundreds, if not thousands, of disciples pioneering new missions all over the world. We want to see people energized, mobilized, and trained to take the nations for the Kingdom of God. I envision a training center here in East Africa for Westerners to receive several weeks of real-world training, and then to go implement what they have learned, either at home or on the foreign mission field. I envision sending our African disciples two-by-two to first African, then Asian, nations, for weeks at a time in search of men of peace. Of course, we would need to have foreign disciples translate our materials into their native tongue. Then they could come to East Africa for extended, in-depth training, returning home strengthened to reach others in their communities. And this might surprise you: I envision no *wazungu* in the field on these missions, but rather indigenous people doing grassroots evangelism, discipleship, church development, and Great Commandment work. A four-phase mission, with an apostle who teaches, manages, builds up from behind the scenes, and then….exits.

But we still want even more laborers. We have found that so very few of our African disciples are carrying the message and mission to their own children. In some cases, it's because our disciples are already older and they no longer have children in the home, or they have lost their influence over adult children. Maybe it's the busy-ness of life as people work so hard, literally for their daily bread. Or, it's the relationship disconnect that we talked about previously. Whatever the reason, it's an impediment to multi-generational reproducibility. After all, in so many Scriptural examples, isn't the man of peace baptized, him *and his household*?

Even for children from a stable home, "the system" owns the next generation through schools. And then there are abandoned children from broken homes and also orphans, all of whom have so very little hope for their redemption. I envision one challenge solving the other: a community of Kingdom-minded families, some, perhaps, taking orphans or foster children into their care, living together and serving each other. Maybe some staff a community school, others cook for the group, and still others have outside jobs. Families can encourage each other in ongoing discipleship (inside and outside the family unit). Through close community living, they will develop deeper relationships with each other and learn to express the unity that is ours in Christ. Those who have means and desire could welcome orphaned children into a true family environment. Just a dream, but…perhaps one day the Lord will bring it to fruition.

If money were no object, these are some of the things we would do, looking forward into the future. Well, friends, money IS no object to our God and King! So will you partner with us in prayer, both for the ongoing work and these visionary initiatives?

> [14] This gospel of the Kingdom shall be preached in the whole world as a testimony to all the nations, and then the end will come. (Matthew 24:14)

Together, we can do our part to usher in the return of our Lord and King Jesus Christ. *Will you join us?*

KINGDOM DRIVEN
ministries

Fulfilling the GREAT COMMISSION and the GREAT COMMANDMENT in East Africa

"Go therefore and make disciples of all the nations, baptizing them in the name of the Father and the Son and the Holy Spirit, teaching them to observe all that I commanded you"

(Matthew 28:19-20)

"YOU SHALL LOVE YOUR NEIGHBOR AS YOURSELF"

(From Matthew 22:36-40; see also Matthew 25:31-46)

Making Disciples

Home Fellowship

Expanding the Kingdom of God

Vital aid for the poor:
- *Job skills and Education*
- *Housing*
- *Funerals*
- *Employment*

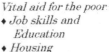

Medical Assistance for the poor

Food for the poor and malnourished

Developing Indigenous Leaders

Glenn Roseberry

The Carrier Family

www.KingdomDriven.org

Appendix A: Pioneer Mission Resources Checklist

So what does a mission look like?

Our field regimen is based on the Great Commission passage in Matthew 28:18-20, Luke 10, and the apostolic model for church development.

> [18] And Jesus came up and spoke to them, saying, "All authority has been given to Me in heaven and on earth. [19] Go therefore and make disciples of all the nations, baptizing them in the name of the Father and the Son and the Holy Spirit, [20] teaching them to observe all that I commanded you; and lo, I am with you always, even to the end of the age." (Matthew 28:18-20)

In line with Luke 10, we strive to identify a man of peace and preach the gospel of the Kingdom. Discipleship begins following surrender, repentance, and baptism. When we are sharing the Kingdom of God, and further discipling the brethren, we utilize our four booklets to insure that the foundations for repentance, baptism, and ongoing discipleship are properly laid. This typically takes place over several different teaching sessions. We start with Lesson 1/book 1, which focuses on teaching about the Kingdom of God; Lesson 2/book 2: Make disciples and baptize them; Lesson 3/book 3: Teach them to obey Jesus; Lesson 4/book 4: Teach about church. During lesson 5, we teach how to stand up a church, starting with facilitating a Discovery Bible Study.

We launch a new Mission by Finding the Man of Peace (see chapter 4)

When we get a leading form the Holy Spirit to launch a mission in a new location, we start with prayer for weeks. This will soften the defenses and prepare the way for our offensive. We then send two disciples, at least one of them being ordained. On-site, they seek the man of peace, listening to the Lord's leading. When they engage the one they discern is the man of peace, they seek an invitation to teach the message of the Kingdom of God, in his home, allowing him to invite his family and neighbors.

Lesson 1: Preach the Kingdom

On first engagement, we preach the Kingdom with a tract we call *The Two Kingdoms*. This booklet takes the candidate from Creation to the Fall, and the predicament of man in regard to sin. Then it explains how Jesus was sent as our redeemer, and through Him, we can be set free from Satan, sin and the world. We introduce the Kingdom message and review many Scriptures illustrating the significance of the Kingdom of God. The book details that man can't serve both Kingdoms but must renounce the one to inherit the other. The book finishes with the prospect having faced clearly the predicament they are in, and the serious decision ahead of them. We then identify those who yearn to hear more and organize the next session. We strictly emphasize that new people are not invited to attend the next session. New people will have to queue for the next wave of teachings. A date and time are agreed upon.

Lesson 2: Surrender, Repent and be Baptized

For the next session, we try hard to be vigilant and only permit people that have attended the first teachings to attend the second. In the second session, we teach a book entitled *Surrender, Repent, and be Baptized*. In this session we cover surrendering to Christ and His Kingdom, what it means to repent, the significance of confession, the purpose and importance of water baptism, the permanence of backsliding, and how to repent practically. In post-Christian parts of Africa, numerous people have already been baptized, yet precious few have ever repented. The teaching explains clearly why repentance is so important prior to water baptism, in order to receive the Holy Spirit. Through these teachings, we (in time) achieve a near 100% baptism rate even for those who have formerly been baptized. At the end of the second session, we bring people to the point of decision. If they surrender, we go through public confession and repentance and baptize them, either immediately or we organize a later time. Upon baptism, the new disciples receive a Bible and we plan the next teaching session. Again, only attendees of the second lesson are invited to attend the third lesson.

Lesson 3: Teach to Obey Jesus

Lesson three is the third part of the Great Commission given by Jesus where He says after baptizing them… "teaching them to observe all that I commanded you." Our third booklet in the series is simply many Bible passages dealing with several often-neglected, practical, and fundamental teachings of Christ. These teachings range from the Great Commandment to the Great Commission and the Judgment, and rely heavily on the Sermon on the Mount. The Beatitudes from the Sermon on the Plain are included in its entirety. Also included are a couple of practical pages of teachings on marriage and divorce, and other family matters. By the time they are finished hearing these teachings, they have been bombarded with what separates Kingdom Christianity from cultural Christianity: that is, the teachings of Christ Himself. This booklet lays a foundation for what it means to be an obedient follower of Jesus Christ. When we finish these teachings, we schedule the next lesson.

Lesson 4: Introduction to Church

The focus of our teachings about church is in book 4, *What does the Bible say About Church?* However, discipleship, church development, and leadership development are all intertwined. In this lesson we detail what the "church" is, where they meet, what they do (interactive Spirit-led service and the Lord's Supper), leadership qualifications, and much more. Much of this has been covered in other parts of this book.

Lesson 5: The Discovery Bible Study

One of the objectives of using DBS is to facilitate a Holy Spirit-led discussion and teaching meetings in the absence of a gifted and trained teacher. Through facilitating the DBS, gifted teachers often emerge and can be encouraged. We hope also to encourage disciples to be reading and applying the Scriptures in their own at home.

Foundational to the Discovery Bible Study is understanding how we are to approach the Scriptures. Let's look at a sample lesson from the DBS on specifically how to read the Bible:

Read Acts 15 and 21:17-25, and Hebrews 8:7-13. What are the requirements for Gentiles as compared to Jews? Were Christian Jews still following the Law of Moses? What about Gentile Christians?

Read Matthew 7:24-27, 1 John 2:3-6, and John 12:47-50. If Gentile Christians are not obligated to obey the Law of Moses, what ARE they obligated to obey? (THE TEACHINGS OF JESUS!)

Read Matthew 7:24-27 again and James 1:22. Did Jesus say to simply obey His commands or act upon His teachings?

Therefore, let us look at how to read Scripture. Start with the New Testament (see Luke 16:16—Kingdom first!).

1.) Read the passage and get to the straightforward meaning (humble yourself like a child; the correct interpretation is that of a ten-to-twelve year old),

2.) Determine what the Lord wants you to get from it and what action He expects,

3.) Just do it!

Here is a controversial yet straightforward example, selected because it is a standalone teaching with no context before or after the teaching:

Read Luke 16:18.

1.) What does it mean? Imagine a twelve year old response. (Yes, it means exactly what it says.)

2.) What does Jesus expect you to get and to do with that teaching?

a.) If married, remain married. If your spouse divorces you remain single to   avoid adultery.

b.) If single, marry wisely because it is a lifelong commitment and do not marry   a divorced person,

c.) If you are married and one of you has been married and divorced prior, repent, because you are committing adultery.

3.) Do a., b,. or c., above depending on your situation!

While teaching the DBS, a facilitator should be familiar with how to read the Bible and should be able to discern the most straight-forward interpretation of Scripture in answers to the questions that are presented. If listeners' answers don't line up with *what the Bible actually says*, or if they show they do not understand the passage in question, the facilitator simply says, "Let's read that passage again." Then, repeat the question and see if understanding is now present. For correct answers, the facilitator may simply ask if anyone else has input to go deeper and finally then repeat the foundational understanding that can be derived from the passage; the review will solidify the teaching for the listeners. We also like to close each session with a reminder to the disciples that the DBS is just a beginning, and that they should continue to read the Bible personally at home.

Why is the DBS so effective for discipleship? We use this activity to introduce the DBS to a group of disciples and explain to them why it's such an effective tool. In a group of people, allow them to briefly glance at a picture of something. Then with the picture hidden, ask them to each individually describe what they saw. They will each cite a small part of it, with others adding a little more detail. Then have them look at it again. Ask one person to explain it. The individual memory becomes the sum of the collective memories. It is the same when "discovering" Scripture. When a person preaches or teaches, each individual only remembers a small part and could never repeat the teaching. But when they discuss it together, their individual memory becomes the sum of the collective memories and they can repeat the teaching. It is a very powerful tool.

Likewise, an individual can teach lies. But a group of people taught (as above) to look at Scripture without bias will be able to recognize and refute false teaching. Do not allow any one, strong individual to dominate and control the lessons. Allow the Holy Spirit to lead and the Scriptures to speak for themselves.

The four discipleship booklets referenced here, as well as other Kingdom expansion resources, are freely available on the KDM Web site, www.kingdomdriven.org/kingdom-resources.

Made in the USA
Middletown, DE
20 July 2016